SPIN

THE ART OF MANAGING THE MEDIA

Nick Clelland and Ryan Coetzee

PENGUIN BOOKS

Published by Penguin Books
an imprint of Penguin Random House South Africa (Pty) Ltd
Reg. No. 1953/000441/07
The Estuaries No. 4, Oxbow Crescent, Century Avenue, Century City, 7441
PO Box 1144, Cape Town, 8000, South Africa
www.penguinrandomhouse.co.za

Penguin
Random House
South Africa

First published 2018

1 3 5 7 9 10 8 6 4 2

Publication © Penguin Random House 2018
Text © Nick Clelland and Ryan Coetzee 2018

Cover photographs © Designed by Rocketpixel / Freepik

PUBLISHER: Marlene Fryer
MANAGING EDITOR: Robert Plummer
EDITOR: Bronwen Maynier
PROOFREADER: Lauren Smith
COVER AND TEXT DESIGNER: Ryan Africa

Set in 11 pt on 15.5 pt Adobe Caslon

Printed by **novus print**, a Novus Holdings company

MIX
Paper from
responsible sources
FSC
www.fsc.org   FSC® C022948

Penguin Random House is committed to a sustainable
future for our business, our readers and our planet. This book
is made from Forest Stewardship Council ® certified paper.

ISBN 978 1 77609 157 7 (print)
ISBN 978 1 77609 158 4 (ePub)

To my girls, Elizabeth and Olweyn
– Nick

To Jessica and Danny
– Ryan

Contents

Introduction 1

1. Building a brand 5
   What you need to understand before
   you even think about the media

2. Practical media skills 19
   Become a professional communicator

3. Driving issues, or how to become famous 67
   Use the media to become a thought leader and
   to build your and your company's reputation

4. Social media 89
   How it can help you build your media profile,
   and how to stay out of trouble

5. Crisis communications 105
   Precisely what to do when it all goes
   to hell in a handbasket

Conclusion.. 125

Appendix: Essential tips...................................... 127
    A quick reference for when you need advice
    on the run

Acknowledgements.. 131

Index.. 133

Introduction

Sex. Drugs. Alcohol. The German conference facilitator took a nervous breath. That was not what he'd been expecting.

It was 1995. The Democratic Party (DP) had been thrashed in South Africa's first democratic elections, claiming only seven seats in Parliament at 1.7 per cent of the vote.

The DP Youth was faring no better. The least important youth wing of the least important party. A ragtag group of student leaders, liberal idealists and youth activists. And the two of us – Nick and Ryan.

The conference had been designed to rebuild the DP Youth, to give it relevance in this new South Africa and to help it find its voice.

We'd all been put into competing work groups tasked with designing a campaign that would get the DP Youth noticed by the media.

Not unexpectedly, there was a group who wanted to

improve education, another with a campaign to create *real* jobs and one with an idea about freedom of the press.

We were put in the same group and it just happened: Sex. Drugs. Alcohol.

A campaign to decriminalise prostitution and marijuana, and to make alcohol available for sale on Sundays.

Relevant – check.

Liberal – check.

Newsworthy – double check.

Needless to say, the powers that be quickly shut down our plans, labelling us troublemakers and pot-stirrers. But that didn't matter. Between us, we had realised that we could, and would, shake up *how* politics was communicated in South Africa. And over the next few years we did exactly that.

Despite and because of the party establishment's resistance to change, sceptical media, openly hostile national broadcasters, scornful and dismissive commentators, contemptuous opponents and treacle-clogged government bureaucracies, we designed and built South Africa's best political communications teams.

This book is about the methods and systems we created along the way, and includes techniques not taught in any communications class or course. Fashioned in the most ruthless media environments on earth, these tools can build your profile and improve your reputation.

If you're looking to learn the deceptive and devious

techniques made infamous in the Gupta/Bell Pottinger saga, then you're going to be disappointed.

This book will teach you how great political communicators maximise good news and manage the bad.

It will teach you the art of managing the media.

But it will do more than that.

You will learn the secret of how to become famous: a simple, counterintuitive methodology that can establish you as a renowned and influential thought leader.

1

Building a brand

*'**Strategy** without **tactics** is the slowest route to victory.*
*Tactics without **strategy** is the noise before defeat.'*
– Sun Tzu

Before we get down to the business of media communications, it is necessary to understand the fundamentals of brand strategy. Otherwise you're on the fast track to becoming the 'noise before defeat'.

There are literally thousands of books and courses on brand strategy, so we're not going to try to summarise all that thinking here. But the basics are simple enough to master easily.

What is a brand? Simply put, a brand is a combination of who you are and what you offer the world. Quite obviously, you won't know what or how to communicate if you don't know the answers to the fundamental questions 'Who am I?' and 'What do I offer?'

DONALD TRUMP 2016 ELECTION CAMPAIGN
Whatever your view of him, Donald Trump's 2016 election campaign was enthralling for millions of people around the world – making it an interesting and accessible case study to explain brand strategy.

Vision

A brand begins with a vision – a picture of the future you seek to bring into being. For the Democratic Alliance (DA), Ryan defined that vision as an 'Open, Opportunity Society for All'. In five words, that vision captured three critical elements of the future the DA was to offer: (1) an open society, underpinned by a constitution that protects people's freedoms; (2) a society in which people have the opportunity – the resources, access and skills – to use their freedoms; and (3) a society in which every person is equal in dignity and worth and deserves a place in the sun.

Visions aren't just important to political parties or companies. They also matter to people. What is the change you want to see in the world? Without a vision, you can't have a purpose, because your purpose, or mission, should be to deliver on your vision.

DONALD TRUMP 2016 VISION
To install Donald Trump as the 45th president of the United States in order to make the US 'bigger, better and stronger than ever before'.

Brand promise

The heart of any brand is a brand promise. A brand promise is exactly that – a clear statement of the value you offer anyone who interacts with your brand. To succeed, a brand promise must:

• Be something you can really deliver.

- Be different from what your competition offers.
- Be something (some) people most want.
- Be easy to communicate.

DONALD TRUMP 2016 BRAND PROMISE
To take back the government from the politically correct
liberal elites (and all they represent and protect) and to
put 'America first'.

The DA won the Western Cape government in 2009, installing Helen Zille as premier. Even with our best intentions, working flat-out, we knew it would be a tough ask to quickly deliver a measurable and noticeable improvement in the lives of every single one of our five million citizens overnight. But we succeeded because we were able to do two important things simultaneously.

First, in contrast to the ineptitude and indifference of our predecessor, we began to actually deliver on our promises.

Second, as that delivery rolled out, we chose a different route to the boastful advertising of other provincial governments, who had spent fortunes on full-page newspaper spreads, TV adverts, in-flight magazine advertorials, radio shows and billboards.

We chose instead to build our programme on one core idea against which we would measure every decision and which citizens could experience first-hand whenever they interacted with government or government programmes.

Developing that idea took a lot of effort, but because it was grounded in the DA's long-established philosophy, we knew where to start. In the African National Congress's (ANC) worldview, the party, via the state, would 'deliver' a new country. In the DA's worldview, the job of government is not to direct and deliver to a passive citizenry. Rather, government's job is to create the opportunity people need to build a better life for themselves. And so, instead of offering people 'a better life', as the ANC had in 1994, we offered a partnership.

In effect, we were going to say to the people of the Western Cape that the offer of a government promising you a better life is off the table. It's not our job to give you a better life. *But* we will make a deal with you: we will give you opportunities to improve your own life. It will be up to you to take responsibility for using those opportunities to actually make your own life better.

A slogan

A slogan should capture the brand promise in a way that brings it to life. Our idea was captured in the words 'Better Together', which we used as the government's new slogan.

In practical terms, it meant:

- We will build you the brand-new Mitchells Plain Hospital and a network of community health clinics, but it is your responsibility to take your antiretroviral every day and make sure that your children are vaccinated. Together, life will be healthier. Better Together.

- We will make sure that your children have the best teachers and schools in South Africa. It is your responsibility as a parent to make sure that your children do their homework every single night. And, if we both keep to our sides of the deal, we will create a great education system and young adults who are equipped for the world. Better Together.

We asked ourselves the critical questions:

Was it true? Yes, our programme in government was designed to create opportunities, from the investment strategy, the education programme, the health service and the partnerships on crime prevention to the approach we took to land reform.

Was it different? It sure was. The ANC's approach was simply to focus on 'delivery', as if citizens are children who need direction and looking after. And of course, when delivery fails, the only one to blame is the ANC itself. Our approach was to treat people as adults, capable of taking responsibility and improving their own lives, given the right opportunities.

Was it something people wanted? We put the effort in here and did our research. It showed that most South Africans don't simply want to be passive recipients of state largesse. They want opportunities, and believe in taking responsibility for using those opportunities.

Was it communicable? By capturing the idea of opportunity with responsibility in the slogan 'Better Together', we could easily explain our decisions and our programme in two words, and on that succinct foundation, go on to explain how what we were doing gave every citizen a real shot at a better life.

DONALD TRUMP 2016 SLOGAN
'Make America Great Again'

It doesn't help knowing all the cleverest communication techniques if you aren't clear about what it is you offer. That's why the first step in successful communication is always to clarify your brand promise, and even better, to be clear about the values that underpin it and the experience you want people to have when they interact with it.

This is true whether you're thinking about your personal brand, the brand of your organisation or the brand of the products or services you sell.

Brand values

A brand's values are what drive its behaviour. Being clear about values is critical to successful communication. More often than not, when leaders or organisations find themselves in hot water, it's because they have compromised one of their values. 'Integrity' is probably the most common brand value in the world, because who wants to engage with a brand that is dishonest? A failure of integrity is also what most often generates the need for crisis communication. As we'll discuss later, when you find yourself in a communications crisis as a consequence of compromising a core value, own it and fix it. You can't spin your way out of a values failure.

DONALD TRUMP 2016 BRAND VALUES
Conservative
Protectionist
Anti-establishment
Honesty – tell it like it is
Trump will never openly admit it, but part
of his campaign's brand values included:
Racist
Xenophobic
Misogynist

Brand personality

A brand personality describes how the brand behaves and who the brand is likely to interact with. Think of the difference between the personalities of Nelson Mandela and Jacob Zuma, for example. Or the difference between Old Mutual and Google.

It's no good wanting to be friendly and engaging if your communication is defensive and angry. How you behave determines the experience people will have of you, and your communication style has to be consistent with your personality or the personality of your organisation. One of the most important parts of your brand personality is that it says what you are not as much as it says what you are. A good, clear brand personality, delivered by the right kind of messages, acts like a wedge. It forces people into a distinct choice.

DONALD TRUMP 2016 BRAND PERSONALITY
Brash
Politically incorrect
Again, he'll never admit it, but part of his campaign's brand personality included:
Authoritarian
Bullying
Aggressive
Bombastic

Communicating your brand promise: on message, in volume, over time

On message

Once you're clear about your brand and what you offer, it is essential to communicate it with ruthless consistency.

There is a golden rule in politics: Stay on message. This is easier said than done. There are a thousand pressures in life and business pushing you off message – crises, great ideas someone mentioned to you in passing, the tediousness of saying the same thing over and over, and the fear that you're getting stale. But think about it: if you don't align all your communication with your brand promise, how are people supposed to know what it is you're promising, and even if they do, how are they supposed to believe it?

Take the example of the Western Cape government. When you have a lumbering government with a R55-billion budget and 80 000 staff, it isn't easy to get every one of your people to communicate the Better Together message every single time they come into contact with anyone from the public.

But that's exactly what we set out to do.

The first thing we did was to turn the message – Better Together – into three steps:

A – What is the **opportunity** we will give?
B – What is the **responsibility** the person must take?
C – What will be the **outcome**, the better life?

From that moment on, every single thing the government did or communicated had to have an ABC or it was vetoed and discarded:

The premier's speeches – ABC
Government events - ABC
Any press statement – ABC
The website – ABC
Radio interviews with officials about the drought – ABC
Announcements about a vaccine day – ABC
Staff magazine – ABC
Team meetings – ABC
Text broadcast messages – ABC

We became obsessed with rigorous adherence to and communication of ABC.

And we know that many inside the government became sick and tired of 'the bloody ABC again'. But that's exactly the sort of discipline you need to take your communication from the mediocre to the excellent. It's only when you and your team start becoming sick and tired about being *on message* that the public hears you for the first time and the feeling begins to take hold.

In volume

But message consistency is not enough. You also have to get it out in volume, by which we mean quantity, not noise. Volume is essential to breaking through the noise barrier of our busy world, competing messages and clamorous lives.

Of course, consistency generates a degree of volume by itself, because at the very least you are aggregating what communication you do put out behind a single message. But there are other ways to achieve volume too:

Volume can be bought. That's what paid communication can do for you. And the great thing is you get to control the message. But the downside is the fact that paying to communicate sometimes undermines credibility. People are alive to being manipulated by advertising, online and off.

Creativity can generate volume. Everyone hankers after the holy grail of 'going viral', and it's great when something does, but the genius of creativity is that it's sticky. People remember things that generate strong feelings.

Multipliers generate volume. Things really take off when supporters or customers start repeating your message for you. It's free, and there is nothing more credible.

Volume can also be generated by 'owning a medium'. If you can't afford to dominate all the channels available to you, pick one or two and dominate them.

Volume is self-replicating, if done successfully. The DA is a good example of this. For years the party had to fight tooth and nail to be covered. It had to scrap for every column inch. But when the environment changed, and the opposition became more legitimate, that same amount of communication started to dominate. It became so successful that the DA is now a reaction machine. It drives very few issues of its own volition. Instead, it maintains a constant presence through reaction. In this way, volume can generate volume, so long as your message is legitimate and credible.

Over time

You can't win a place in people's hearts and minds overnight. That's why it's necessary to stay on message over time. If it's the right offer, it won't need to change in any event. But the temptation to chop and change is ever present. Sure, there are times to refresh a brand, but it should only be transformed if circumstances have changed so fundamentally that the offer is no longer relevant. The best example is probably Coca-Cola. It's been offering the same thing – the ultimate in refreshment – for decades. Sure, the packaging has been tweaked and the slogan refreshed, but the offer hasn't changed. That's staying on message over time.

Being true to your own values – a lesson from Bell Pottinger

It's all fine and well communicating your vision, values and brand promise if they are aligned to ethical standards and decent human behaviour. But what about those who seek to communicate with nefarious or unethical intentions? It would be naive in the extreme to assume that the techniques and strategies we share with you here are only ever used by those with principled and decent intentions. The PR firm born in 1987 out of a union between Margaret Thatcher's spin doctor Tim Bell and Piers Pottinger – Bell Pottinger – was one of the international giants in strategic communications. Working on contracts for the now notorious Gupta family in 2016/17, they infamously used these techniques and communications skills to actively incite racial tension and sow discord in South Africa as the spin doctors of 'state capture'. They developed a brilliantly insidious message – 'white monopoly capital' – laced with just enough truth and emotional resonance to act as the perfect counterpoint to any criticism levelled against the Guptas, their corrupt endeavours, and any politicians and officials caught up in their web of deceit. And with an army of fake Twitter accounts and apparatchiks for hire, they were 'on message, in volume, over time'.

In this instance, their behaviour caught up with them. In September 2017, Bell Pottinger was found to have breached ethical standards and brought the PR industry into disrepute. The resultant scandal saw the disgraced firm expelled from its professional body and almost immediately put into administration. In one fell swoop, Bell Pottinger – the company and its brand – was completely and irrevocably destroyed. While this was a victory of sorts for the good guys, a lesson to take from this saga is that it is important to always bear in mind that your opponents (be they ethical or otherwise) could very well be using the exact same techniques that you are.

2

Practical media skills

In April 2002, Nick was in Johannesburg for the week preceding the newly formed Democratic Alliance's first national congress to be held at Nasrec. His job was to brief editors and senior journalists on the direction and strategic intent of the new party – background information they could use to contextualise the upcoming events and speeches that weekend at the congress.

It was around 5 p.m. in the afternoon and Nick was at the congress venue watching the backdrops of the new logo and slogans being erected. 'They're going to look great on TV,' he thought when his mobile phone rang. It was a call from the party's senior leadership in Cape Town: 'All that we know right now is that there are allegations that [former DA premier and then Cape Town mayor] Gerald Morkel had an "inappropriate relationship" with a German confidence trickster by the name of Jurgen Harksen.' Nick took a breath, knowing what was coming. They continued, 'You're going to have to deal with this as national spokesperson. You can say we will investigate and follow all normal procedures, but that's about it – just be vague.'

It was 6 a.m. the next morning when Nick's phone started ringing. In the days before online news, he had already been driving around Kempton Park for 20 minutes with fellow member of Parliament (MP) Mike Waters, desperately looking for a copy of the *Star* newspaper with the story on the front page.

John Perlman, the bearish host of AM Live on SAfm, was on the line. Sitting next to Mike with the paper open on his lap, Nick manfully answered all Perlman's questions and allegations, trying to be as sincere and sound as trustworthy as possible under the circumstances. Perlman was wrapping up when he stopped Nick mid-sentence: 'But with due respect Mr Clelland, you are being vague.'

According to Mike, who was doing the driving and quietly listening to all this unfold, Nick fist-pumped the air and let out a barely audible 'Whoop!' At that moment, most of South Africa thought he was a slippery little bugger, but he had done what had been asked of him. Because, sometimes, just surviving the media onslaught is winning.

The professional political communicator

'Media skills training' courses where former journalists and PR types teach skills to the uninitiated are now commonplace. A bit like tourist tandem-skydiving adventures, you learn a few skills and get to feel the thrill of the real deal. But what does it take to be an elite military para-trooper?

Working in environments where even the people who actually like you treat you with scepticism – and where your opponents wake up every morning intent on destroying you – political communicators are the toughest and most successful communicators anywhere. And every political media team we've been part of has always done the same four things better than anyone else:

1. Built real relationships with important journalists and editors – the forgotten skill that can make all the difference.
2. Understood the nature of news – particularly from the journalist's perspective.
3. Proactively created news – for when you *want* to be in the media.
4. Been expert at reactive communications – what to do when the media contacts you – including damage limitation.

Relationships with journalists and editors

Somewhere along the line, amid all the tips, tricks and theories about media communications, people forgot about the humans involved. The systems and the techniques took over. And when relationships are left unattended and uncared for, the consequences are always negative.

If we were a couples' counsellor advising anyone on how best to have a meaningful (read: effective) relationship with a journalist, we'd tell you what you'd probably expect to hear: make a sincere effort over time, BUT in a carefully measured and objectively managed way. Hardly the stuff of hearts and roses and, sure, more calculating than you might want to consider for a romantic relationship, but it is what you need to do … and it works.

The DP (and later the DA) had always based its relations with journalists on the personalities involved. This leader was friendly with that journo. That journo really admired this politician. This provincial leader once had a massive spat with that journo so they were kept at arm's length.

In summary, the party had generally good relationships with journalists. But a modern political party can't just leave something like that to chance and to the lottery of friendship and conviviality. What we needed was a management system. So we created a thing with the grand title of Media Relationship Management Programme – basically a simple spreadsheet with the name of every journalist, editor and producer in South Africa deemed important to our interests.

Next to their name was the last time we had met them and how that meeting had gone, in a few words. Each journalist was given a designated minimum regularity of contact for somebody from the party to see them – face to face and usually without any particular matter to be discussed. (As this tool has evolved over time, newer versions are updated with what they are saying or thinking based on their Twitter and Facebook posts and an analysis of their latest articles, etc.)

This deceptively simple, even rudimentary tool produced dividends. Journalists with bugbears or specific issues were quickly identified and placated. Those with negative or unfavourable dispositions were fed the sort of stories that might change their thinking over time – or were simply managed as best as possible. Outright haters were watched for any infringement of the press code, which was either dealt with immediately or filed so that – if necessary – we could prove animus over time.

We appreciate that the very nature of this system undermines what many understand to be the true meaning of a relationship. Sure, we spent many hours with people we personally do not like or would ever want to be friends with. In those instances, both parties knew the drill. But there were many more wonderful human beings we met and got to know through that process – some of whom are today our closest friends. It is the nature of humanity. Taking the time to meet with a journalist – over a meal or a cup of coffee – always takes the relationship to a personal level of some sort. Whether it's the small talk about your kids or just gossip and intrigue, or even an honest and sincere haranguing, meeting face to face builds an interpersonal relationship. And if done with respect and honesty, it allows each of you to get to know the other as a human being.

When things go wrong, as inevitably they will (a scandal, an attack or a problem), and that journalist calls you, they know you and hopefully at least respect you. So that when you push back, saying, 'Listen, this is not cool because of this, this and this' or 'I can assure you, this is all rubbish' or 'I just can't get it for you now, I need an extra day', they believe you and are far more likely to entertain your requests. These are the peacetime investments that pay dividends during the war – it goes without saying that if you haven't invested by that stage, it's far too late to start trying.

You may not need to run an extensive, nationwide Media Relationship Management Programme, but you do need to work on your relationships with journalists. At the very least, we'd suggest anyone interested in a media profile should:

- Compile a list of every local journalist who has written or spoken about your area of interest or subject.
- Research those who haven't but who might be interested in you.
- Read everything they write; listen to their radio shows. (Actually, read as much as you possibly can on your subject regardless.)
- Establish some media credibility in your area (a series of letters to the editor, an op-ed article, a newsworthy media release), then ask to meet for a coffee with the editor or journo.
- Send them useful information or insights as you come across them (but do not spam them with your every

waking thought, and keep a watchful eye out for cues that you might be overdoing it).

- Try to see them as often as seems right for your context.
- Don't just see them once and then never talk to them again.

It is often important that a journalist know something without having to say who told them. If you watch Sky News carefully, you'll be amazed how often they predict 'The prime minister is expected to be announcing this new plan tomorrow' or 'The leader of the opposition is believed to be outraged by the announcement and will be challenging the prime minister on this in Questions tomorrow'. How do they know this stuff?

Professional political communicators decide what would be good for journalists to know in advance for two main reasons: firstly, to get the media to speculate that you are going to do something, and then to actually cover the something when you do it. This gives your story two bites at the proverbial cherry. Clever.

Secondly, if they aren't given some background information and context before an event or announcement, they'll have to speculate on the reasons, motivation and rationale for it. Sometimes they'll be correct, but sometimes they'll be dead wrong. Incorrect speculation is usually messy and distracting, and certainly always off message.

These 'grey area' types of communication are, ironically, governed by a set of fairly black and white conventions and rules relating to the information conveyed in chats with journalists:

'On the record': anything said can be quoted and attributed directly to you. All conversations with journalists are considered 'on the record' unless you specifically say they aren't. This includes conversations and chats outside of a formal interview or over drinks or even when you bump into them at the supermarket.

'Unattributable': anything said can be reported but not actually attributed to anyone. In practice, people rarely use this convention – it seldom works in the interest of either the journalist or the communicator. The more popular and oft-used variation of this is 'Chatham House Rule' (or what in South Africa is often referred to as 'Lunch Time Rules'). The UK's Royal Institute of International Affairs, commonly known as Chatham House, introduced this rule in 1927: 'When a meeting, or part thereof, is held under the Chatham House Rule, participants are free to use the information received, but neither the identity nor the affiliation of the speaker(s), nor that of any other participant, may be revealed.'

'For attribution as ...': anything you say can be quoted directly, but you must agree in advance to how you will be identified. For example, 'a senior source in the president's office' or 'a party insider'.

'Off the record' or 'background': What you say and the

information you provide is to be used by the journalist only to give them context or background or a unique insight into their reporting. They can't publish any of it at all.

In reality, you may never use or need these conventions … until that one particularly messy situation or complex crisis or tense stand-off, and then knowing them could very well be the edge you need to get the coverage you desire. Or perhaps simply to survive.

It is important to know that the conventions aren't covered by the Press Code (and you can't refer breaches to the ombudsman), but in all our years we have never met a single journalist who doesn't honour them. Even if you discount the fact that most journos are genuinely good people, it simply isn't in their interests not to honour them.

In the heat of national elections, spin doctors like us spend their days doing 'off the record' or 'background' briefings. Nick's job – as DA director of communications – was to go and see every editor, producer and senior political journalist in the country at least two or three times during the three-month campaign. He crisscrossed the country, drinking endless coffees, talking to them about the ideas behind the campaign – why we're doing this or campaigning against that, and perhaps even giving them a bit of internal party gossip, the sorts of things that keep those meetings mutually beneficial. While most were held over a cup of coffee or perhaps even a lunch, there was one particular meeting that stood out.

Nick was to meet with the editor of a major national newspaper and he knew the timing of the meeting was awful: hours before the paper would be put to bed – crunch time for any editor. Nick figured in advance that the meeting had been scheduled purposely at that time to keep it short. However, as he sat down with the editor, someone arrived with a tray of crystal glasses and matching ice bucket followed by a bottle of expensive whisky. Three hours later, Nick stumbled out of the editor's office hoping he hadn't revealed too much as the whisky took hold and wondering how on earth the newspaper would look the next day – as it turned out, that particular edition of the paper was a winner.

Sometimes, however, constructive relationships just aren't possible, irrespective of the effort you put into them. DA MP Geordin Hill-Lewis loves to remind Nick of his first day in Parliament as a young intern. Apparently he was sitting in the party's research office when Nick stormed in, mid-tirade on the phone to the head of news at the SABC: 'Snuki, I honestly do not give a fuck. If you do not send a camera, I will hit you with every fucking legal and political weapon I can find!'

Obviously the relationship had reached a point where the SABC were being openly hostile to the DA. And Nick was simply doing what was necessary when the national broadcaster refused point-blank to cover our campaign launch despite televising the ANC's live. It was drinking in the Last Chance Saloon – somewhere we hope you will never have to drink. (The SABC did eventually send a camera crew to our event. They scanned the room for empty chairs and white faces and finished off their insert with an analysis from the ANC that, incidentally, was longer than the clip of us that preceded and provoked it.)

Cultivating a good relationship with a journalist requires honesty. Too many politicians have made this mistake and paid dearly for it: lie to your partner, lie to your best friend – but never lie to a journalist. Sooner or later they will find out and they will never trust you again. If you can't tell them something, then tell them that you can't. If telling them something implicates you, then tell them that too. Just don't lie.

Poor reporting is unfortunately part and parcel of South African journalism for a number of complex reasons that need not be elaborated on here. Suffice to say, you should watch for the following, among others:

- If you are inaccurately quoted or referenced;
- If you are edited out of a story you are responsible for identifying or breaking;
- If other comments or facts are inaccurate; and
- If a story is biased when it should be objective.

There are a number of remedies you can use to rectify an inaccuracy. More often than not a newspaper will publish a letter or opinion piece correcting the facts. If they refuse to do so, each paper has an ombudsman who can be approached, and if they refuse to act, one can approach the South African press ombudsman. Only take these latter two action steps if your case is watertight.

If you begin to notice that a particular journalist is regularly problematic, the first rule is never to go straight over his or her head. We live in a world where we are quick to 'call the manager' or 'report you to your boss'. But as US congressman Charles Brownson famously said, 'I never quarrel with a man who buys ink by the barrel.' Sure, you might win this particular skirmish, but that journalist covering your beat will be at their desk tomorrow and you will have made an enemy. If you have a problem with the journalist, tell them. Say 'this is a problem', ask 'how do we fix it' and try to work it out. Only once you've tried your best to no avail, can you say to the journalist, 'This is not good, who can I talk to?' or 'I'm not happy with this, I'm going to your editor.' Always make every effort to sort it out with the journalist personally first.

Things you need to understand about journalists and the nature of news before you get going

Before we can even contemplate trying to make news, it's important to understand how things work from the *journalist's perspective*. While we cannot claim to be able to give definitive insight into journalists, there are some important things that politicians in particular seem to continuously misunderstand – or just miss – about journalists and the work they do:

- Journalists have particular interests and passions. Not only do they tend to specialise (for example, in legal, political or environmental journalism), but they also each have their own interests *within* their specific fields. Often journalists will run with one story (or in one direction), so choosing who to direct your attention to matters.

- News cycles are critical. Getting a story online or hard news in a daily or a weekly story in a Sunday paper requires knowledge of deadlines and how to influence them. Even daily deadlines can make or break a story. And each type of medium requires a different approach. With Sunday newspapers, for example, as Sunday approaches, spaces fill up in a certain order: the op-ed page first, hard news last, with the most sensational news the very last. So if you have a humdinger, it's sometimes a good idea to wait until the Friday before giving it to a Sunday paper, thereby 'forcing' the paper to carry your story more prominently and nearer the front.

- Controlling copy and subediting is possible, sometimes. Where possible, it's a good idea to ask to see proofs of a story, especially when you run an op-ed or give an interview. Subeditors have a different agenda to reporters. They seek, effectively, to drive impact. That can often see important information edited out.

- Know who to turn to in the hierarchy. Understanding how a media house is structured is important. Every journalist reports to a section editor, who in turn reports to the editor. Sometimes journalists make the wrong call about a story's importance and it is necessary to elevate your concern. Knowing who to call is critical. But always be upfront and honest with a journalist before going over their head.

- Understand recourse. Know how internal ombudsmen and the press ombudsman work and their importance. Likewise, get to know and understand the norms and standards of the various media outlets.

- Understand the context. No journalist sees your organisation, your message or your press release as particularly important – and certainly not as important as you do. It is one of a thousand messages they receive every day. So do not flood them.

- Understand their markets and their reach. An interview on SABC is totally different to one on eNCA. *Business Day*'s readership is a particular demographic of aspirant business leaders. The *New Age* is generally not read by anyone with a critical or independent perspective on current affairs. The *Sunday Times* has far more readers than *City Press*, etc.

- Play different media off against one another. A good story is a powerful tool. Sometimes it's better to offer an exclusive (or at least a *first-use* exclusive) to one newspaper instead of sending out a 'spray and pray' general press release to everyone. That way you are almost assured of much more prominence than you ordinarily would have received. This might mean having to hawk your exclusive around to see who's prepared to offer you the best deal. Just remember, this is only for really big news – it's the exception, not the rule.

- Understand their politics. Different media houses have different priorities, both in terms of specialisation and values. A story on state-owned enterprise debt restructuring is going to have much more chance of getting into *Business Day* than the *Sowetan*. Likewise, a pro-DA story is more likely to get into *Die Burger* than the *New Age*. At the same time, it is helpful to try to understand the broader media context and the general narratives that underpin any particular message. Jacob Zuma was always a universal issue anyone could tap into. What the DA is doing in Johannesburg does not enjoy the same level of interest.

The relationship from the journalist's perspective

We asked senior journalists to tell us what they want from politicians and anyone else they must communicate with professionally. Here is an amalgamation of their views. (Any repetition of points covered elsewhere in this book is entirely on purpose – the points need to be made.)

Honesty

The most important aspect is honesty. In the end, your good name is all you have. It is free, but it is also priceless. Guard it above all else. Once squandered, it can never really be regained.

When a crisis arises you must manage it, but be sure not to lie, to mislead or bullshit. Journalists are not stupid. They have long memories and they hate being made fools of by the disingenuous. You may succeed once, but you will pay the price forever.

These days, it has become commonplace for bribes or sweeteners (known as 'brown envelopes' in the trade) to be offered by the powerful, especially when they are under pressure. No journalist worth his or her salt will even countenance accepting a bribe. So if you were to offer a brown envelope, the type of journalist who may accept it is one you don't really want to associate with, and those who won't – the vast majority – will never deal with you again.

If you mess up, admit it and then work hard and honestly never to make that mistake again.

Availability

If you regard yourself as being in public service, it means you must be available to the public as much as possible. This includes being available to journalists. The most trusted and respected politicians are those who never lie and, perhaps even more importantly, are the ones who pick up their phone and engage with journalists in a decent manner as fellow human beings. If they cannot speak at that moment, they will endeavour to call the journalist back – and they invariably do – within a specified timeframe, or they will ask the journalist to call them back at a specific time and then are actually available (in other words, the initial delay is not kicking for touch).

If they do not have the required information, they will refer the journalist to someone who has, always confirming their own availability if that person is impossible to reach. Or they will access the information themselves and call the journalist back directly.

A communicator must be able and available to communicate. If not, the journalist will find another source and write you off.

Brevity

Answer the question put to you and don't extrapolate or repeat endlessly. The journalist will ask more questions if he or she needs more answers. Get to the point. Then stop.

On/off the record

We deal with on and off the record information else-where in this book. Be sure to know the difference between completely on the record, completely off the record, on the record for attribution and on the record not for attribution.

Make it clear *before* every point if it is off the record. You cannot give a journalist a lot of information and then claim afterwards (even directly afterwards) that it was given off the record. By the end of the conversation, you and the journalist must agree and be clear on which information is on and off the record. Some of the worst disagreements between journalists and sources are on this point.

If you master the skill of communicating on and off the record, you will have attained one of the most impor-tant skillsets imaginable. It builds trust between you and the journalist, and it helps you craft your message. This trust is a precious resource not to be squandered or used expeditiously, because it is finite. Always be worthy of this trust – if it is lost, it can never be regained.

Knowledge

Always know what you are talking about. In other words, do not fly by the seat of your pants. Put in the long hours of research on your subject until you have mastered it to the point that talking about it comes naturally to you. This requires you to be curious about your subject. You must care about it. If you do, your passion will shine through.

One of the worst things is a public figure speaking about something he or she is not knowledgeable on. One example was in November 2017 when South Africa's deputy minister of public enterprises, Ben Martins, was accused in a parliamentary hearing of meeting with members of the odious Gupta family. Martins called a press conference, only to reveal that he could not remember where he was on the day in question! His hard-won credibility was in tatters by the end of it.

If you do not know the answer to a question, own up. Don't waffle, lie or provide incorrect information. Rather say something like: 'That is an excellent question. I cannot answer at the moment, but I'll get back to you' or 'I cannot recall the precise information right now, but I'll provide it to you in the next hour'. Then keep to your undertaking and provide that answer.

Press releases

Press releases need to be brisk and to the point. Sentences must be short. Do not use more than three sets of statistics. A good press release must include an action step.

Always be available if you are the contact person for the press release. Few things frustrate journalists more than receiving an interesting press release on a fresh or breaking story, only to find that the contact person cannot be reached.

Always know exactly what the press release says and a bit more, so that the journalist doesn't think you are just an automaton repeating the press release they have already read.

If information is required that you do not know, find the information as soon as possible and give it to the journalist.

Press conferences
When you send out a press conference media alert, see that it is done timeously. The place, time and topic of the press conference must be stated clearly.

Be at the venue on time and start on time. Waiting journalists are irritated journalists.

Have a chairperson to provide variety, and to handle questions and maintain order.

Take questions either one by one or in batches of four, and answer each one.

Don't let any one journalist dominate a press conference. Give everyone a chance.

Finish the press conference at a specific time. Don't let it drag on indefinitely.

When you answer, be to the point and take more questions. Journalists will ask what they want to know.

Respect and good manners
Always respect the journalist. Do not become angry. Remain dignified, professional and friendly, because tomorrow you will have to work with that same journalist again.

Proactively creating news

So you want to be in the media? Well, the first thing you have to do is tell the world about the thing you believe is newsworthy (we'll discuss how to create newsworthy content later). And there are many ways to do this using various media platforms/mechanisms:

- TV or radio interview
- Press conference
- Tweet
- Facebook video
- Photo op
- Speech
- Media event
- Press release

This list isn't exhaustive – you are only limited by your creativity. All of them are self-explanatory and not particularly bound by any rules. But unless you are Donald Trump (he'd tweet it) or President Ramaphosa (he'd make a speech) or Richard Branson (media stunts are his bag), in the day-to-day South African context you are more likely to make use of the press release.

So seeing that it is the bread and butter of all communications, let's explore the characteristics of a good press release.

Writing a great press release

A press release should always be the consequence of careful thinking long before you type the first word. Specifically, these are the sorts of things you should be thinking and the questions you should be asking:

- What is the newsworthiness of what we are saying?
- If we communicate this position or news, what are we telling the public about us as an organisation – or me as an individual?
- Is what we are communicating in line with our value proposition?
- What is the best way to communicate this message in a manner that both relays its importance and is of news value?
- Is a press release the media mechanism most likely to effectively communicate my message?

All of these should inform the answer to a final question you should always ask:

- What is the story I want to see in the media as a result of this press release?

Only once you have considered these questions and concluded that there is an issue of importance and news value, and that a press release is the best way to communicate your position on that issue, does it become necessary to actually draft a press release.

Once written, a useful test of a good press release is

to take a step back and look at the language used and ask the following questions:

- Are the words simple and easily understood?
- Are the sentences short and coherent?
- Are there any sentences or phrases that can be cut or simplified to make the writing – and thus the message – more focused and direct?

Here is an example of an overly complex sentence:

> The repeated criminal activities of those responsible for governing the police department are compromising its ability to properly interrogate its own affairs with the result that most internal cases are not being considered and managed in a timeous and effective manner.

Written more simply, we could end up with something like this:

> Rampant corruption of senior police officials means the department can't do its job properly. As a consequence, most internal cases are not being completed.

A long-winded and complex sentence is much more effectively and powerfully expressed in two or three shorter sentences. And there are many other benefits to this approach. Chief among these is that shorter sentences are more quotable, or more 'media friendly'.

A journalist is far more likely to use the second version, because it lends itself to a short news story. Each sentence is both coherent and quotable, as compared to the long and tortured sentence above.

Structure

A good press release has a specific structure which, if used, makes it much more likely to effectively convey its message to the media and, importantly, to the public.

This structure is designed with the media in mind. Because the purpose of a press release is to talk to the media, your statement should make the media's job as easy as possible.

The opening paragraph of a statement must always explain three things:

- What the news is;
- What our position on that news is; and
- Why this is important.

There are two reasons for this. Firstly, the media is flooded with information every day and any press release needs to be able to explain its purpose immediately and effectively if it is to stand out among the many other competing stories. Secondly, a good press release will be used by radio, and radio presenters do not have the luxury of editing stories to ensure they cut to the chase – news bulletins are built on short, pointed summaries of the key facts. A first paragraph that can achieve this will go a long way towards increasing its chances of being covered on radio news.

We always put a red pen straight through any press release whose first sentence (or opening paragraph, if we're feeling charitable) ignores the three vital questions – usually in favour of some long-winded attempt to set the context or, worse, justify what is to come.

Once you have a good opening to your press release, you need to elaborate on it. The body of a statement gives you space to provide three things that the opening does not:

- Argument and analysis
- Context
- Evidence

These three things are of critical value to any press release and, as far as possible, any press release should contain all three. Also, and significantly, each cannot appear on its own.

An argument is necessary because this is how you present your case. If you do not have an analysis or a frame of reference, then you do not have an opinion or position and your press release is nothing more than a news story.

Linked to this is context. Context allows you to link any issue to a broader theme or trend; in other words, to the bigger picture. This has the double effect of bolstering the weight of an argument and increasing the statement's news value, because few stories are placed in their proper context, but are rather reported on in isolation.

Finally, there is evidence. Any sound argument must be based on evidence. An argument without evidence or context is simply an opinion.

Other features of a good press release

Title: The title of a press release is crucial. A good press release has a short, punchy and accurate title. It should identify the news and your position in a few words. It needs to be interesting – it needs to grab attention – but it must also be accurate.

An example of a bad title:

> The Minister of Safety and Security should consider reinstating specialised units to combat gangsterism

An example of a good title:

> Minister ignoring solution to gang violence

Action step: Some press releases need an action step. An action step is an undertaking to actually do something that allows you to drive an issue further. Any action step is a process, and a process has a life of its own. As that process unfolds, it generates more opportunities to comment further on the issue.

Tone: A good press release should be written in a tone that is appropriate and measured. It must never be hysterical, patronising, superior or damning. The trick is to express the appropriate reaction to the issue at hand. For example, if someone has been brutally murdered, that is suitably described as 'shocking'. However, if a national department misses a deadline, that is not 'shocking'. It is better described as 'disappointing' or 'an indictment'.

Statistics: Statistics are a powerful way of increasing a press statement's impact. They allow you to translate language into numbers and present information in a far more persuasive form. Also, statistics are more objective than mere words: they create the impression that the information is indisputable, which bolsters the credibility of a press statement. If you have a statistic to supplement an idea or a view, that view becomes far more authoritative.

Statistics should always be presented simply and clearly – as often as possible they should be in table form and they should illustrate the central point being made in the statement. And they don't need to be limited to numbers. Graphs work well too. Any way of making a point in a visual manner that stands out from the language that surrounds it and attracts the reader's eye to that particular piece of information is a powerful addition to a piece of communication.

A good final rule is to read over the press statement and ask: Does every sentence in this directly impact and strengthen the prospect of the story I want publish? If it does not, if it is vague, detracting or repetitive, it should be cut.

Selling your press release

Once upon a time, media officers in our parliamentary offices thought that drafting a good press release and pushing 'send' was all they needed to do before settling in with a cup of tea to wait for the odd follow-up question or arrange an interview or sound bite. We put an end to that laziness and yet we are always amazed at how many organisations still do it: 'We issued a press release and no one picked it up,' they'll tell us. 'Who did you sell it to?' we'll ask, only to be met with blank stares.

When you de-romanticise the idea of your important press release and accept that it's just another email filling up a journo's inbox, you begin to understand the importance of selling it. The second a release was sent, we had our media officers start contacting journos. And we're not talking about a glorified telephonic version of the prompt 'you've got mail'. Drawing from their relationships with and understanding of various journalists' fields of interest and emphasis, they would have quick chats designed to pique interest and get the journo engaged in the issue. Perhaps they'd offer the journo something exclusive (i.e. not in the press release) – information we'd specifically held back or a snippet of context not widely known – or they might even offer to send through photos or evidence – anything that brings the story to life and makes the press release more likely to be published.

Selling an important press release is not an optional extra. It is a necessary and vital part of the process. Some press releases sell themselves – they are intrinsically news-worthy. 'Selling' is therefore typically reserved for those media statements that do not immediately make a massive impact; those that are for the record or that don't excite or aren't dramatic, but are nonetheless important. We don't recommend selling *every* statement. If you did, after a while journalists won't be able to distinguish importance from standard communication and it will begin to work against you.

A quick note about multiple press releases: One of the things the DA quickly became known for was the huge amount of press releases we were issuing every day of the week. Our drive and enthusiasm wasn't being met with the same sentiment on the receiving end. Journalists couldn't deal with the volume and started deleting them on arrival. That's when we took a decision to cap daily press releases at no more than three per day unless something particularly dramatic happened. Nowadays, however, that rule seems to be under strain.

Media alerts

Media alerts for events are also critical. You want your major announcements, news events or unveilings to be well attended. This means that your media team must do more than issue a media alert informing journalists of the event. They must manage the operation, from explaining its importance to confirming attendance, ensuring photographers and TV crews have been booked and dispatched, and getting all the important bums on seats on time. During the actual event, they must ensure that journalists get copies of the speech or press release, and that they get good access and an opportunity to interview the key speaker exclusively afterwards if needs be.

Scaling it up

There may be some of you who work in large, complex and multifaceted environments wondering whether any of these tips and techniques can work on scale. The answer is yes.

The Western Cape government employed 70 000 staff across all the province's schools, hospitals, retirement and nursing homes, police departments, road construction camps, etc.

When Nick arrived as the newly appointed director of strategic communications, each department and ministry (housed in 20 different buildings throughout the Cape Town CBD, with some even in Stellenbosch) simply did their own thing as far as the media was concerned. They acted as independent entities without due consideration or thought for any other unit or department. This all changed abruptly when he instituted a daily media meeting at 8:30 in the premier's office with every professional communicator in the government as well as ministerial spokespersons.

In this 30-minute daily slot we analysed the media coverage we had received in the last 24 hours and decided what needed responding to or rebutting, selected what other opportunities arose from the coverage and noted trends, both positive and potentially negative. The second half of the 30 minutes was spent on proactive communication. Anyone who wanted to communicate that day – be it a media release, an event, a photo op or a launch – was put onto a planning and permissions grid to prevent overlap, to spread our media coverage across entire weeks instead of competing with ourselves for media on one day, and to actively search for synergies and opportunities for collaboration.

In this way, an entire government was kept on message, responsively nimble and opportunistically proactive.

Online news media and why you need discretion, tact and experience

It wasn't that long ago when political parties planned all of their media activities around what is called the 24-hour news cycle. In the DA – in the precursor to the Western Cape government's system – we'd meet first thing in the morning to analyse the morning newspapers and radio news bulletins as well as the previous night's TV news. From this we could identify opportunities for new things to say as well as decide what needed responding to as a matter of course. This also gave us a good indication of the best time or day (with clear space and no one else contesting for headlines) to release our own news in the form of press conferences, announcements or policy documents. As a rule we'd always try to get all of our press releases for any given day out before noon so that all of the newspapers would have time to include them in their processes for the next day's editions. When those newspapers hit the streets at dawn, radio stations would be the first to pick them up and run with them – and if the story had 'legs', TV would pick it up later in the day for that night's news.

Those days are over. Now every newspaper, radio and TV station in South Africa has an online presence. Add to that digital platforms like *Daily Maverick* and *Politicsweb*, not to mention the power of social media (we discuss this later) and the fact that more South Africans get their news from their timelines than from newspapers, and you can see why the idea of a lumbering 24-hour news cycle is a thing of the past. News can break at any moment, day or night, and spread at the speed of a click.

Online news (and social media) is an incredibly volatile and dangerous medium, and, at the same time, incredibly powerful. It tends to drive hysteria, not news. Here, the most experienced and effective communicators are the most discerning. They have learnt that sometimes it's safer and more strategic to step back and not dive in head first, particularly as a fast-moving story develops.

The problem, though, is that politicians are under enormous pressure to keep up or risk becoming irrelevant. And they are under constant pressure to communicate immediate moral outrage or make some sort of pronouncement as news breaks. They become willing captives of an inescapable vortex when they subscribe to being available to comment and respond to news as it happens.

Exacerbating this response is a credible fear that the news they are planning to make or the comment or analysis they want to give might be scooped by someone else or, worse, will already be obsolete. There are more than enough examples that demonstrate how online's insatiable desire for content rewards politicians who make the effort to speak first or, far better, produce their own news or analysis.

The high-risk/high-reward approach of some politicians is best suited to the mavericks and troublemakers. In your business and personal communications, you likely do not need to move at this pace and, frankly, neither should thoughtful politicians. Knowing when and how to use online media requires tact and judgement, much of which comes from experience.

There are quirks particular to this relatively new media for which you should always watch out. Seemingly inconsequential news can suddenly become the next major story if it happens at a quiet moment in the news cycle. The speed of this news cycle – which is more of a constant news onslaught than a news cycle per se – also means that stories can come and go within hours and, in some cases, the best way to handle a bad-news story about yourself is simply to sit tight and wait for the next story to eclipse it.

The online-media lessons to take from this are:

- You need to know what is happening in your field all the time. Set up alerts or use apps that will notify you when relevant and import news breaks.
- If you have decided to say something quickly, make absolutely sure you are both correct *and* adding value to the story (then ask yourself whether you've considered all unintended consequences).
- If you have news, take care to release it before someone else does.
- Use news-cycle quiet times to release your news to give yourself clear space.
- Consider delaying your news if the news cycle is too cluttered.
- Create unique and interesting thought leadership as often as you can.
- Most importantly, don't get caught up in the frenzy. Take the time to carefully consider whether jumping right in will help or hinder.

Beyond the press release – creativity and ideas

Before we got into press releases, we mentioned alternate media mechanisms like interviews, tweets and media stunts as ways of getting your message to the world. Most of them are self-explanatory or at least easy enough to research for yourself. What is much more difficult to explain or teach is lateral thinking and creative alternatives.

If communication is the marketplace of ideas, then

creativity is one of its strongest currencies. And yet few ever speculate with it.

Instead of droning on about the various elements of creativity or giving you a set of pointers on how to be creative (all of which are futile), here are a few creative things we've done over the years to generate media attention and to communicate our message:

A day in the life

Concerned that DA leader Tony Leon seemed out of touch with the ordinary South African, we built a programme where he spent 'a day in the life' experiencing the life and occupations of various South Africans, including a nurse, a police officer, a street vendor and a steelworker. He'd spend an evening with them, commute with them and work alongside them. The media loved it – TV, radio and print all covered the campaign in glorious technicolour detail.

Chicken suit

Stolen unashamedly from 'Chicken George' (a campaign tactic in the 1992 US presidential election, where people dressed in chicken costumes heckled President George H.W. Bush over his refusal to participate in a debate with Democratic candidate Bill Clinton), we dressed up the then young activist – and now DA chief whip – John Steenhuisen as a chicken to shadow New National Party leader Marthinus van Schalkwyk for two weeks at all public appearances, claiming he was too afraid to face the voters after joining the ANC. It was a big media hit.

'Fire Manto' bumper stickers

Our campaign to get Manto Tshabalala-Msimang fired as minister of health was given a boost after we made bumper stickers stating 'FireManto.co.za' and had MPs hold them up in solidarity during a sitting of Parliament. The resultant outcry (it broke parliamentary protocol) and debate it generated were covered by CNN, among others.

Playing cards (of shame)

Another direct crib, this time from the 2003 invasion of Iraq, where the US military developed a set of playing cards to help troops identify the most-wanted members of President Saddam Hussein's government. Our version was a deck of playing cards that highlighted the candidates on the ANC election lists who had 'betrayed their office as public representatives'. President Thabo Mbeki appeared as the Ace of Hearts, identified as the leader of the AIDS denialists in the ANC. Health minister Manto Tshabalala-Msimang appeared as his Queen of Hearts for being a 'committed AIDS denialist and flouter of court orders'. We even found a place for Marthinus van Schalk-wyk as the Joker. TV loved this one.

Post-box to Parliament

Our research told us that people felt Parliament was isolated and out of touch with ordinary life. So we created a campaign called 'Post-box to Parliament', giving people the opportunity to email or write to us about their issues.

That alone would've been a fairly ordinary idea, so we built a giant red post box and literally placed it on the front steps of Parliament. Tony Leon opened it up and read messages from the public. Needless to say it not only created huge media attention, but also led to a flood of correspondence from people we could help or connect with.

Durban Poison
During the 1996 local government elections, a comedy show decided they'd spoof our DP election posters with their own 'DP = Durban Poison' posters. Their posters closely resembled our design and quite soon the Mrs Grundys began to complain. When contacted by the media, we could've gone for the classic 'rebuke' or 'ignore' approach, but we offered the journalist another option. We suggested a joint photo of them with their poster and Nick with ours, side by side, and an article about the ker-fuffle. Nick was careful to make sure the story that ran disassociated the party from Durban Poison (marijuana) but also demonstrated our ability to laugh at ourselves. The *Sunday Tribune* article was a sublime success.

Controversial billboards
The DA has long used billboards as a relatively quick and cheap way to generate media coverage. Often booked for the short 'downtime' periods between long-term corporate campaigns, the costs of the production and flighting are almost always eclipsed by the TV, radio and other news

coverage of the billboard itself. One campaign of billboards erected on the N3 and N1 highways in Johannesburg read: 'E-tolls. Proudly brought to you by the ANC.' These garnered massive, nationwide media coverage and debate.

How to respond (or react) to the media

One day your phone will ring or an email will pop into your inbox:

> Hi, I'm Jane Doe from the *Bugle* – I just
> wanted to chat to you about what you said at
> that neighbourhood-watch meeting last night.

Or worse: your phone will be ringing off the hook – texts, WhatsApp messages and even Facebook messages will light up your screen like the proverbial Christmas tree.

What do you do?

First contact

In the movies, a journalist will contact you for a face-to-face interview in a smoke-filled room, or invite you to a glitzy TV studio or to the radio station for a live interview. This almost never happens in real life. What usually happens is a journalist calls you on your mobile phone and says, 'I want some information' or 'Tell me about this, this and this' or 'I'm doing a story about that', or they'll say, 'I'm phoning for a sound bite for the 2 p.m. news bulletin'.

The first thing to do when they call you is to buy time. So when they call you out of the blue and ask to speak to you, ask them if you can call them back. This will give you time to formulate a position or response.

If they're from a newspaper, ask them to email the questions to you. Journos don't particularly like this, but it works and they will do it. Do not answer questions on the phone. Emailed replies are much safer and more effective because:

- You can carefully choose your words, particularly with complex or difficult subjects.
- Often what you think are intelligent and well-thought-out verbal responses are rambling streams of consciousness.
- Somebody else can check and – if necessary – sign-off your written responses.
- You have a record of what you've 'said'.

Tip: Always send less information than they ask for. If it's the kind of article where you might ordinarily get one or two sentences in at best, don't send them three paragraphs leaving them to choose the one they like. Rather send them the two best sentences you have and force them to use those, particularly if they are writing about something you've done wrong or about a criticism of you, and when your impulse might be to explain yourself – perhaps in painstaking detail, perhaps as long as a whole page. The next day the article will only have one sentence from you and it'll be the sentence that doesn't particularly help your cause. Remember: explaining is losing. Always give them as little as possible – and then they have to use it.

If they're from a radio station and are calling you for a sound bite, buy some time to prepare and get your head straight. Just say you need some time, even if it's only 10 minutes. This gives you a few moments to get your message right and to rehearse potentially tough questions (more on how to handle these later).

Stay on message

Stay on message, in volume, over time. Always remember the message. Every question you answer is an opportunity to re-communicate the message. During the 1992 US presidential campaign, Bill Clinton's lead strategist, James Carville, wrote 'The economy, stupid' on the board at the Clintons' Little Rock campaign headquarters. Initially intended as a reminder to keep the campaign team 'on message', their message discipline was so successful that the phrase became a de facto slogan for the Clinton campaign.

Read every one of the quotable sentences you want to send to the journalist. Are they on message? If not, why not?

Keep to the deadline

Depending on who they work for and their medium, journalists are all on different deadlines – radio might want your sound bite for the next bulletin, the online site may want your comment for a story that's going up now and the newspaper might need a comment by 3 p.m. to make their print deadline.

So when a journalist calls you, always ask them when their deadline is.

It is possible to try to push the deadline, but to attempt that you have to know how their particular media works. What time in the morning do they meet to discuss the day's stories for their newspaper? What time after lunch do they start producing the paper and make their editorial decisions? What time does the paper go to bed? In other words, what time does the paper get printed? There are deadlines and then there is the hard deadline (there's even another deadline past that, but to 'stop the press' you'd better have huge news). If you don't know these things you can't push deadlines. Sometimes you might want to say to the journalist, 'Listen, hold the story for today. I know you want the story, but I'll give you something really worthwhile for tomorrow.'

There are different techniques you can try, but ultimately it's all about the relationship with the journalist – if it's built on honesty and credibility, you will always have a better chance. That said, always adhere to their deadline once you have made the deal. Don't break that promise.

Advanced radio/in-person interview tips

So they've actually asked you in to do an interview or they are going to call you for a telephonic interview. You've asked for some time and you've been given it. Now what do you do?

The first thing you have to do is prepare responses and practise them. By practising we do not mean running through them in your head. Actually say the responses out loud. There's no point in thinking your responses to the journalist or writing them down. Practise the actual talking bit. Perhaps have someone listen to you. Once you've said it a few times, and you know it's correct and on message, then you're ready. Practice is not writing, practice is not thinking, practice is talking out loud.

You must cover all the controversial areas ahead of the interview. So if you know something's controversial or problematic or sticky, make sure you have an answer to the worst possible question they could throw at you. Don't pretend it's not going to be asked. Force yourself to answer the most difficult possible question. And do it out loud. When you can deal with that, everything else is easy.

Find out who will be interviewing you. Knowing their character and personality will help determine the type of interview you might have. Sometimes you will face an aggressive interviewer (Kieno Kammies in full stride); at other times your interviewer will be friendly and warm (Redi Tlhabi). If you know who they are and how they will likely be, it's a big help in preparing for your interview.

And feel free to compliment a good question or insight from the interviewer.

Also check that no surprise guests will be sprung on you, or whether you are on a panel or on your own.

Find out how much time you will have, particularly if you're going to be interviewed live on the radio. There's no point in settling in for a 15-minute fireside chat and it's over before you can get your feet up. Always ask for the exact allotted time. If you have 30 seconds, you know you can only get your message in there two or three times, so do it. If you've got 10 minutes, you can pad it a bit and get your message in there 10 times.

Of course we're not advocating that you don't answer the questions put to you and that you simply rabbit off the message – that would be absurd.

But there is a trick that we call 'drag and drop'. Let's say you want to talk about a new education system, but the interviewer insists you discuss trade unions, so you say something like: 'Trade unions have been battling to retain members and relevance for years now – save for the South African Democratic Teachers Union, where they are the bane of our educational system and the reason why we need to introduce this new educational system …' Straight back to your message. Drag and drop. You are not there for a picnic. You are not there to have a friendly chat. You are there for the message and only the message. Not for your fame, not for your popularity, not because your friends can say you did so well. It's all about the message.

Be passionate and be yourself (hopefully 'yourself' is passionate). Don't be fake, don't be someone you're not, don't try to be too intelligent or too philosophical or too anything you aren't. You must be yourself.

Tip: In call centres and radio stations around the world, trainees are told that you can *hear* a smile. Try it for yourself. If someone is smiling, you can hear it. So, when on radio, force yourself to smile.

Then there's the anatomical issue of the ratio of mouth to ears. Too many politicians inverse the ratio and that's where mistakes happen and arrogance breeds. Listen carefully to what the interviewer asks you and take your time. Try not to immediately jump to the pre-prepared rote answer you've rehearsed without thinking carefully about whether it will answer *this* question.

Tip: If you don't know the answer immediately, and you want to buy a second or so more to think, say, 'Sorry, I didn't hear that, could you repeat your question please?' Sure, you heard it clearly the first time, but sometimes those extra seconds give you the space for an infinitely better response.

If you don't know the answer, say so. Do not make shit up. Too many politicians have got into trouble for making stuff up because they felt pressurised: they're an important person live on air, surely they should know the answer to this, so they make it up. Don't do it. It is more authentic and more credible to say, 'You know what, I don't know the answer, but I'll find it out and I'll come straight back to you.'

Journalists also have techniques they deploy to get you flustered, to get you to make mistakes. Our all-time favourite of these tricks is called 'filling the silence'. Imagine you're on a date with somebody that you've just met. You're having a candlelit dinner and you're talking, each taking turns, and then the person supposed to go next just says nothing and stares at you. In that awkward moment of silence you feel compelled to say something more – to perhaps add to what you've already said or to bring up something new – all in an attempt to prevent social embarrassment and awkwardness. And that's what some interviewers do. They wait two beats after your reply to see if you can be cajoled into saying something you hadn't anticipated. And when you eventually say something, it's the wrong thing because you're nervous. Don't fill the silence. Rather smile and suggest you could talk more about the message.

Another technique they may try is to use aggression or to scold you: 'But this is completely unacceptable, why have you done xyz…?' Just be calm – be empathetic to their frustration and express understanding, but take them back to the message.

Other techniques include:
- Relentlessly repeating themselves, perhaps rephrasing the question, to gain information you may not want to give ('Ask one question at a time, please').
- Asking what may seem to be inappropriate questions ('I'm afraid I'm not prepared to answer that question').

- Interrupting you mid-thought or mid-sentence ('Just give me a moment to finish my point and then I'm all yours').

Finally, having a sense of the public mood on the issue beforehand is essential, irrespective of your side in the debate.

Tips for TV

If you are invited to go for a television interview at the studio, say yes to makeup. Far too often you see men in particular sitting in TV interviews looking like big glistening balls of sweat. And that immediately makes them seem untrustworthy. The first-ever televised US presidential debate pitted a sweaty and uncomfortable-looking Vice President Nixon against a calm and confident-looking Senator John F. Kennedy. The irony is that radio listeners thought Nixon had won the debate, but the TV audience (more than 80 per cent of Americans were watching) overwhelmingly believed that Kennedy had won.

The way you sit and your posture affect how people respond to you. Sit up, shoulders back, and lean forward a little – it gives the effect of appearing engaging. A trick for those who wear jackets is to pull the back of it under your bum and to sit on it so it pulls your shoulders into a good posture.

Always ask what or who you should look at: the camera or the interviewer. Usually you will look at the interviewer, but it's a strange, unreal environment with a TV camera, bright lights and other crew members surrounding you, so your eyes tend to wander to them. The effect of this is to make you look either like you're on drugs or that you are untrustworthy. So if the journalist says, 'Look at me', you've got to actually focus on the eyes of the journalist for the duration of the interview – beyond the point where it becomes uncomfortable.

There are times when they will ask you to keep your eyes only on the camera, and that's a little more difficult. We often do TV interviews for eNCA, whose newsroom is based in Johannesburg but who has a studio in Cape Town. So you sit in this studio with three cameras and bright lights in your face, an earpiece in your ear to listen to the interviewer … and not a soul in sight. Just an empty room and one red light to watch for when the camera is live. And when it goes red you've got to focus on that light and engage and smile and be animated as if the red light were the person talking to you in your ear.

It goes without saying – more so than on radio – that smiling and displaying a friendly demeanour makes you more engaging on TV. You might have a moment when you need to be tough or mean and say your thing, but people like someone who can smile, someone they can imagine chatting to themselves.

One last technical point is to avoid the strobe effect: clothing with checks, stripes or patterns that make TV cameras go berserk. Once, Nick accompanied then Western

Cape minister of transport Robin Carlisle to a TV interview, and to his utter horror he had to strip off his business shirt in front of a full TV studio for Robin to wear, as his own pin-striped shirt was producing a strobe effect. Lesson learnt.

3

Driving issues, or how to become famous

There are names that everyone just knows. These instantly recognisable people have used their celebrity and reputations to establish themselves as leaders in politics or in their respective industries and – off the back of that – have grown successful careers. People like:

- Richard Branson
- Julius Malema
- Tim Noakes

And while they may have been born with the gift of a personality that generates celebrity and reputation, the fact of the matter is that if you have passion, credibility and integrity you can do the same – if you know how.

We created a system for politicians that can transform anyone into a major thought leader. We place them at the centre of campaigns designed to demonstrate their credibility and leadership, and, importantly, we take those campaigns directly to the mainstream media – where their competitors wouldn't even dream of appearing. This gives them the sort of competitive advantage that paid PR and advertising cannot hope to emulate.

Ryan conceptualised this system – called 'driving issues' – in the 1990s, at a time when the then Democratic Party was a 1.7 per cent triviality and couldn't rely on the media to cover even a major announcement, never mind a daily press release.

And boy does it work. But there is a catch: you're going to have to be more Donald Trump than Hillary Clinton. More Julius Malema than Lindiwe Sisulu. More Tim Noakes than Michael Mol. In other words, if you are conflict averse, forget it. This isn't for you.

The beauty of the system was in commodifying and operationalising the seemingly inherent charismatic newsworthiness that comes naturally to gifted communicators and demagogues alike.

When training politicians, we always use a classic South African example. During apartheid, Raymond Ackerman's Pick n Pay sold petrol at 12 of his stores, where he was subject to the petrol price regulation of the day. Contemptuous of this stranglehold on prices, Ackerman began offering food vouchers with the petrol sold at his petrol stations. Naturally the government was apoplectic at this upstart who dared to challenge their rules. He was threatened, vilified and condemned. And all of this conflict happened in the full glare of the media. Big, juicy conflict. And conflict equals news.

In the news he was Raymond Ackerman, the businessman fighting for cheaper fuel against a law with which he disagreed. But for South Africans who read about him or listened to him on the radio, he was fighting for them and for their families.

Ackerman lost his fight with the government, but that he fought at all earned him the nickname 'the housewives' friend', something his still-developing retail business, Pick n Pay, was happy to accept. The lesson to take from this is that it takes bravery and a willingness to incite a conflict of ideas to build a profile this way.

The problem today with any business, non-governmental organisation or politician who wants to get noticed is that they tend to be less like Raymond Ackerman and more like Ronald McDonald – all flash and no substance: tweets, photo ops and anodyne corporate PR-crafted press releases.

Here's an everyday corporate communications scenario: You think of something to say, something great or wonderful you have done. 'We've achieved this,' you say proudly, or 'We're making this important announcement' or perhaps, if you're really edgy, you complain about something bad or terrible someone else has done: 'We are shocked at her behaviour', 'We are reporting him to the ombudsman' or 'We are going to press charges against them'. Then you write a press release and send it out into the world. And at best you get a bit of coverage that fizzles out after a while; at worst, only your friends and family retweet you.

Why? Because you are boring. And your press releases are boring too.

A client once complained to Nick about how years ago he'd made a mistake, crossed an ethical line, and it was carried in the newspaper. 'Ever since then,' he complained, 'I have done my best to be a more than model citizen, I've done good things, I've helped charities, I have worked tirelessly against corruption and nobody ever writes about it despite all the press releases I send out. And when they do write about me they refer to me as Mr X, who did that bad thing once.' And that's how he's known, not as Mr X, who now does wonderful things, because everything that he's done since has been, by comparison, boring. It's been good, but it's been boring.

And everyone is doing the same thing. Modern communications has evolved into a PR sausage factory, mass-producing boredom and triviality. A daily production line of perfunctory press releases, smiling-face photo opportunities and announcements heralding the next tepid cup of weak tea. It's all wah-wah-wah and fades into the noise the second you press send.

If you want to be noticed you have to break through the noise and competing self-promoting mediocrity, and get your message to the most important place in communications. This is at the centre of driving issues; you have to get your message to that place. So what is the most important place in communications?

The family dinner table.

No, we're not kidding. The family dinner table is the holy grail of effective communications. If you make it to there, you've made it everywhere – literally.

Think about your family sitting down for a meal:

'Goodness gracious, what did you think about that new economic study on the environmental sustainability of haddock?'

Or:

'I'm so relieved that ABC are serious about economic development. I was concerned they weren't, but luckily their 1 200 word op-ed put me straight.'

The examples are ridiculous and unlikely, and yet these are precisely the kinds of conversations your press statements and media events are (futilely) hoping to generate every single day.

If your family is anything like ours, they are more soap opera than soap box: 'I can't believe James did that' or 'I don't want to gossip, but Kate has been doing it for six months without telling anyone!'

People talk about what people are doing. And when they do talk about the world outside the people they know, it's more like: 'I don't care, I'm not paying for tolls' or 'Can you believe the president wants another new jet?'

They don't discuss the abstract or the theoretical or the mundane. So why does your press release?

When made to consider whether your press release could be spoken about at the dinner table, you are forced to reconsider every single part of it. And if you do this fastidiously, it will begin to improve your hit rate. But if you want proper, sustainable coverage in the media, then hold on – we've only just begun.

Sure, there will always be a place for what we call 'rote' press releases, comments and tweets. These are usually to respond to news, to make announcements and to herald good things you might have done. So let's assume that they will continue as per normal. What won't, however, is everything else.

If you are serious about making a name for yourself in the media, you're going to have to rethink everything else you communicate.

At the epicentre of driving issues is the differentiation between what we call a theme and an issue.

Almost every politician we've ever worked with has told us that they are against corruption, are anti-crime or are working towards improving education. Big whoop. We always say to them: 'But your opponent *also* wants less corruption, your opponent *also* wants less crime and your opponent *also* wants better education.'

So how do you distinguish yourself? You can't. That's why you've got to move away from these general areas (what we call themes) and focus instead on a specific question – something we call an issue.

Simply put, a theme is a general area of policy. Crime is a theme, health is a theme, social development is a theme, sustainability is a theme. An issue is a specific question that relates to the theme. For example:

Theme	Issue
Education	Fire non-performing school principals
Health	Incentivise HIV testing with lotteries
Environment	Ban plastic shopping bags

Issues are effectively stories to which people can relate. They should be told like stories that unfold over time. Each chapter of the story should briefly explain what happened last and situate the latest developments in that context. Stories should all move towards a conclusion: the moral/purpose or desired outcome behind making it an issue. For example, a campaign to fire non-performing school principals should move towards an outcome where children receive measurably better education, giving them more opportunities to succeed in life. So issues/stories should have a sense of momentum and progress (see the seven-point checklist for driving issues below). This is what keeps the story moving and compelling. Through it all, people relate to you – the person telling the story/campaigning for the outcome/driving the issue. As the storyteller, you are their surrogate. You are actually telling a story about the reader, not about yourself. The right (or wrong) stories can define you for life. People remember stories. The more relatable they are, the better.

The seven-point checklist
for driving issues

Creating and leveraging conflict is the core concept at the heart of driving issues. Over the years, we've established a checklist – or a set of seven rules – that, if followed carefully, will guarantee you an exponential increase in your media profile and the resultant boon for your brand.

1. Stay on message.
2. Make sure there is a binary position.
3. Select the correct opponent.
4. Is there real conflict?
5. Be first.
6. Protect your issue from theft.
7. Make sure your issue is sustainable.

1. Stay on message

The first rule is that your issue must be on message. An issue that does not specifically reflect your brand promise and values will undermine it instead – muddying all of your communications. For example, if your brand promise is about 'excellence in education', you wouldn't campaign to lower the pass rate for mathematics.

2. Make sure there is a binary position

Secondly, the issue must have a clear binary position. Yes or no. For or against. There must be no grey area. To be 'a little bit for' or 'a little bit against' or to have 'relatively good reasons despite some compelling counterarguments' means that it is not an issue. Either you are for the president spending money on the Nkandla upgrades or you are against it. Either you are for a wall between the US and Mexico or you are against it.

3. Select the correct opponent

The third requirement for a good issue is a formidable opponent. Ideally, your opponent should be of a higher (or at least equal) status than you. To choose somebody lower in status or less significant than you is to bestow your status on them by engaging with them in public. (By status we are referring to their public profile and standing on the subject your issue relates to.) Also, you could just seem like a bully. And always choose an opponent who either has a good media profile or wants one. They must have an appetite and a predilection for debate, argument and counterpoint. Someone who simply ignores you – whatever their status or importance – is the wrong kind of opponent. If you're battling to conceptualise what I mean, simply think Fikile Mbalula.

When he was an MP, Ryan famously went all the way in picking his opponent when he asked then president Thabo Mbeki during a parliamentary debate whether he believed the high rate of sexual violence in South Africa contributed to the spread of HIV, and whether the president believed HIV causes AIDS. Mbeki responded by accusing Ryan of succumbing to the 'disease of racism', but avoided responding directly to the question, which, in turn, reignited criticism of his government's response to the pandemic.

4. Is there real conflict?
Always make sure that there is conflict in your issue – in other words, pick a fight. But test this objectively, with someone outside of your own dinner table.

5. Be first
It is critical with proactive issue-driving to be the first to define the issue. This not only helps you define the parameters of the issue itself, but also the subsequent debate. Critical to 'owning' an issue – so that it becomes synonymous with you – is being first. From there, you need to be central to breaking news on the issue going forward. If you break it, you tend to own it. The value of this cannot be underestimated. You can take over someone else's issue, but it is incredibly difficult and requires double the amount of work. The arms deal is a great example. The work the DA did on the arms deal over the 2000s was unparalleled. But everyone remembers then Pan Africanist Congress MP Patricia de Lille, who stood up in Parliament and revealed all the initial information. To this day it is part of her brand. That is the kind of power being first has.

6. Protect your issue from theft
Just because you thought of it first, or because you have worked hardest in a field, doesn't mean you have an

ordained right to own any particular issue. Always guard against your issue being stolen. For more or less two years, the DA owned the campaign against the Nkandla upgrades. They revelled in press statements, marches to the gates of the homestead, and parliamentary questions and motions. Then in May 2015, the Economic Freedom Fighters (EFF), an upstart 'revolutionary socialist' party led by expelled former ANC Youth League president Julius Malema, caused unprecedented chaos and disruption in Parliament chanting 'Pay back the money' directly at President Zuma. Their actions may have crossed a line in terms of parliamentary procedure, but the media coverage was prolific and the issue almost immediately transferred party-political ownership – from the DA to the EFF – in one fell swoop.

Your personal issue may not be at the heart of the national public debate, but there will always be somebody who wants to jump on your bandwagon. The only way to protect the ownership of your issue is to do two things simultaneously: make sure you are the most credible and vocal proponent of your side of the issue; and never stop looking for new opportunities to sustain the conflict, and the media attention.

7. Make sure your issue is sustainable
This brings us to the last rule: working tirelessly to make sure your issue is sustainable. Sure, some great issues are time and place dependent – they explode and then they

are done. But ideally, you want to keep an issue alive for as long as possible – for months, if not years.

Examples of driving issues

Let's start with an example from the 2016 US presidential election related to the theme of illegal immigration and its consequences for Americans. Pushed for a simple yes or no, it would've been difficult to imagine that either Hillary Clinton or Donald Trump would've been in favour of illegal immigration. In other words, they agreed on the theme. But Trump had an issue.

Announcing his candidacy in June 2015, Donald Trump said: 'I will build a great wall – and nobody builds walls better than me, believe me – and I'll build them very inexpensively. I will build a great, great wall on our southern border, and I will make Mexico pay for that wall. Mark my words.'

Whatever your views on immigration, it's hardly the thing – as a concept and a theme – that comes up for discussion at the dinner table.

But people certainly spoke about Trump's wall at dinnertime. Personally, you might be for a wall or dead-set against one. But everyone knew about the wall because of Donald Trump.

Theme: illegal immigration
Issue: a wall between the US and Mexico

Closer to home, corruption is seemingly always in the news. It's the perfect example of a theme, not an issue.

Although people are frustrated and angry about corruption in general, it's hardly sustainable for any sort of dinner conversation in its generic form:

'Don't you just hate all this corruption, Mary? Pass the salt please.'

But if Gupta 'state capture', Hlaudi Motsoeneng's qualifications or Nkandla come up, people get talking. Take Nkandla for instance, the scandal over the R246 million of public funds used to make improvements to the president's private home, ostensibly for security reasons. As if not sexy enough as an issue, the upgrade included a perfectly normal suburban swimming pool officially designated a 'firepool' because it could be used as a source of water for fire-fighting.

Theme: corruption
Issue: public money spent to upgrade Nkandla

The point about selecting the right issue to campaign on is that it positions you on the theme. If you want to be known as the person who fights corruption, don't tell everyone you are against corruption, and don't make speeches that rail against corruption, because they will fade into the background the second your microphone is switched off. Rather, mount a fight against the Nkandla upgrades: demand justice, initiate investigations. That will not only show people that you are a warrior against corruption, it will also demonstrate that you are out there, in the trenches, fighting on their behalf.

That's precisely what the DA did with Nkandla. Their then parliamentary leader, Lindiwe Mazibuko, led a massive campaign that included laying complaints with the Public Protector, demanding parliamentary oversight and sanction, and marching to the doorstep of the homestead itself.

The response was precisely what the party had hoped for. The government and the ANC steadfastly defended the upgrades and the president. When one person says one thing and somebody else says the opposite, you have conflict. And conflict generates news.

We have already explained how an issue is a specific question that relates to a theme. But it is also more than that: it is a metaphor for a theme – a powerful story that captures and embodies all the public emotions and intellectual concerns of a theme. The more emotional the issue, the more powerful.

The various DA campaigns against luxury ministerial vehicles and their bullyboy blue-light brigades are a great example of this. Taking an emotive issue (everyone has been pushed off the road by blue lights), the opposition DA defined the ANC government in negative terms (arrogant and self-indulgent) and illustrated corruption (the theme) in a powerful, simple way that everyone could understand. They also, and this is an important point, gave the issue an extended lifespan by prolonging the story: each time a minister bought a new car, every time someone was forced off the road by blue-light bullies, when DA Western Cape ministers removed the blue lights from their vehicles, and so on. Ultimately, though, its greatest attribute was that it was a wedge issue – something that split the ANC: while some within the ruling party would have agreed that spending extravagantly on luxury vehicles was obscene, Zuma had built his nepotistic regime on patronage and the perks of office. He could never clamp down on them and he could never defend them as good or necessary. It had all the characteristics of a perfect issue.

Theme: corruption
Issue: luxury ministerial vehicles with blue lights

Think about the most-read articles on your favourite news site or about the front-page headlines in any Sunday newspaper: conflict is news; kumbaya happiness is not.

The notion that conflict generates news is the epicentre of driving issues. Seemingly obvious and self-evident, it is famously absent in the majority of press releases that make the daily journey from your computer to the journalist's inbox and on to their trash folder.

Driving issues doesn't just make politicians famous

either. The concept works universally and in any environment. Here are examples of South Africans who have successfully been driving issues for years:

Zachie Achmat
Theme: HIV/AIDS activism
Issue: Refuses to take antiretrovirals until they are freely available to all

Wayne Duvenhage and OUTA
Theme: High-handed government decisions
Issue: Refuses to pay for e-Tolls

Ian Player
Theme: Nature conservation – save the rhino
Issue: Supports legal rhino horn trade

Brett Murray
Theme: Freedom of expression
Issue: Paints *The Spear* – a Leninesque depiction of President Zuma with his penis exposed

Raymond Ackerman
Theme: Petrol price regulations
Issue: Gave food vouchers for Pick n Pay with petrol purchases

Another example is Tim Noakes. Once a niche long-distance running expert and author of *Lore of Running*, Noakes has become world famous as the primary advocate for a low-carbohydrate, high-fat diet known as Banting.

The diet has attracted doubt and even condemnation from some doctors and dietitians concerned about the risks of a diet rich in animal fats and relatively low in vegetables and fruit. The Health Professions Council of South Africa processed a complaint of misconduct against Noakes too, but Banting continues to grow in popularity, perhaps because people actually do lose weight on the diet. The conflict between those for and against Banting, coupled with the credibility of seeing people lose weight, has propelled Noakes to a new level of stardom – it would not be an overstatement to suggest that he has become the personification of Banting and weight loss for many South Africans.

By now, the paradigm should be clear:
• Ordinary comment is ordinary.
• Good news is boring.
• Conflict is news.
• So, pick a fight.

We have purposely used dramatic examples to illustrate our points. But driving issues is not limited to mega issues on the national or international stage. Anyone can do it in any environment. You can do it in your business or in your community too:

- A citizen who campaigns for people *not* to give food or money to homeless kids;
- A businessperson who calls for an increase in VAT;
- A resident who campaigns to ban dogs from the local park;
- An online company that disrupts older, established ways of doing things;
- A doctor who prescribes and campaigns for e-cigarettes to smokers;
- A cyclist who campaigns for people not to have to wear helmets;
- An organic egg producer who takes on the big egg-producing companies;
- A parent who takes a stand against a unanimous decision of a PTA; or
- Nick, the young MP who went face to face with a president over a jet.

Shortly after the 1999 general election in South Africa, DA leader Tony Leon called Nick, then a young, fresh-faced MP, into his office. There were whispers that then president Thabo Mbeki was going to buy a brand-new luxury jet. 'Your job is to become Mr Jet,' he said. That was all the encouragement Nick needed. But before he could even contemplate going public with the DA's position on the purchase, he had to understand the subject – he had to make himself credible.

So he found out all there was to know about the proposed jet. It was to be a Boeing Business Jet (BBJ), a corporate luxury version of the standard Boeing jet airliner you'd use to fly from Cape Town to Johannesburg. Nick researched the purchase price, running costs per nautical mile, servicing costs, crew requirements, maximum range and minimum runway length. He became an expert in all things aviation, compiling all the information and banking it.

Then he looked for other jets with a similar range that might be cheaper. He identified the Bombardier Global Express and Gulfstream V as viable cheaper alternatives, and compared their purchase prices, technical specifications and other operating costs to the BBJ, and banked that information.

Taking another tack, he found out which heads of state didn't have private jets – at the time, these included the leaders of Britain, New Zealand, Canada and Greece. Banked.

Nick then compared the price of the US president's Air Force One to South Africa's proposed BBJ as fractions relative to the respective countries' GDPs and banked the calculation.

Using previous annual schedules, he calculated what it would have cost to fly the president for a year exclusively using the first-class cabin of South African Airways (SAA) and compared that to the costs of the BBJ. The results were not surprising, and he banked those too.

All of this preparation and hard work did two things:

it made Nick an expert on all things jet-related, giving him credibility, and it allowed him to build an arsenal of information that he could use – piece by piece over time – to sustain the conflict and his issue over months and years.

When he was sufficiently prepared, Nick launched his campaign with an irreverent question directly to the president in Parliament: Why was he buying a jet when South Africa had so many other pressing needs? Mbeki fudged the answer, but the deed was done. The media whipped themselves into a frenzy over the conflict between the young white opposition MP and the venerable black president. And just as soon as that hype began to subside, Nick had a press release ready about operating costs, followed a week later by an op-ed on cheaper aircraft, followed by a media event about how SAA first class would be cheaper … you get the idea. A continuous barrage of new information to sustain the issue. Thanks to the minister of defence, the South African Air Force and the Presidency all rushing to defend the purchase, oodles of conflict and – consequently – media coverage followed suit.

Months passed and every time Nick said something about the jet, it was seen as both credible and newsworthy. It got to the point that every time he spoke in Parliament, he'd be heckled with taunts of his exact initial brief: 'Here's Mr Jet!' Mission accomplished.

On 20 October 2002, just minutes after midnight, a luxury jet landed at Waterkloof Air Force Base outside

Pretoria. Seven hours later, Nick sat down at his desk in Parliament to read the purposely bland one-liner from the air force announcing the arrival of the presidential BBJ, to be named *Inkwazi*. 'Clever bastards,' he thought. He'd been so looking forward to pointing to the jet as it landed – in front of the amassed media – the final act in the drama he'd starred in for more than a year. But this was clever – bringing the jet in under cover of darkness in the wee hours of the morning. Nick googled the name *Inkwazi* – 'African Fish Eagle', it said. What followed was one of the shortest press statements he'd ever write – simply titled 'The Ego Has Landed'. The wall-to-wall coverage of his statement that followed had less to do with his clever wordplay than with the fact that he had come to personify the feeling – held by many – that this luxury jet was wasteful and inappropriate.

It's relatively easy to understand the paradigm and the checklist of rules for driving issues. What is far more difficult is to actually find an issue that fulfils all of these criteria – but they are out there if you are willing to put the effort in to finding them. To find them you must become a hunter of issues. Every day, you must read the newspaper, watch Twitter and other social media, listen to the radio, and keep a finger on the pulse of what's going on in your society, all the while looking, brainstorming, checking and testing for issues against the checklist. Once you have one – an issue that meets every requirement of the checklist – you have the equivalent of the media holy grail. It will make you famous. It will grow your brand and reputation. Who knows what it could do for your business?

4

Social media

@realDonaldTrump: The [US] has great strength & patience, but if it is forced to defend itself or its allies, we will have no choice but to totally destroy #NoKo.

@helenzille: For those claiming legacy of colonialism was ONLY negative, think of our independent judiciary, transport infrastructure, piped water, etc.

@Julius_S_Malema: The children of the black nation should take a stand, is now or never. We want our Land now

Twitter and politicians. Not since fire and oxygen has there been such a perfectly combustible relationship. On social media, the three 'A's of communications disaster – arrogance, aggression and access – line up like a missile guidance system sending political communicators into damage-control mode.

According to the South African Social Media Landscape Report for 2018, South Africa has 16 million Facebook users, of which 14 million access the internet from their mobile phones. Around half of that number are on Twitter, while Instagram boasts a little less than four million South African users. These are formidable numbers and precisely why politicians have decided that the rewards far outweigh the risks.

Messages direct to their markets

Once held hostage by the vicissitudes of media coverage, politicians can now duck the cameras and microphones and speak directly to you – and they do, in all their unedited and subjective glory. When you consider that Helen Zille and Julius Malema have more than a million Twitter followers each, and even the anodyne official Presidency account has more than 920 000 followers, you can see the impact it has. Twitter, in particular, is now regularly used as the quickest and most effective way for politicians and parties to rebut opponents and clarify issues.

Politicians are becoming their own 'TV stations'

It's not only Twitter. Angela Merkel's federal government YouTube account features news-style TV interviews with the German chancellor, who gets to explain her decisions and policies to convivial and compliant interviewers. Back in South Africa, the DA did much the same with leader Mmusi Maimane's *Bokamoso* video blog and regular Facebook videos of their politicians taking on the ANC in Parliament. When you consider that Facebook's timeline algorithm is geared towards promoting video content – and particularly native Facebook video content – there's no doubt that this is just the beginning and we should expect to be bombarded with more and more video content from politicians and campaigners in future.

Social media is winning elections

Political campaigns now routinely use social media to reach their audiences, with consumer data and demographics gathered by social media networks like Facebook – who ordinarily use it to sell the products that 'appear' on your timeline. So in as much as you are likely to be bombarded with shoe adverts after buying shoes online, if you can be deemed to be a 'religious conservative' then expect to be bombarded with messages that appeal to your spiritual beliefs. One of the many infamous, allegedly Russian-bought, Facebook ads from the 2016 US election was used to show that Muslim women supported Hillary Clinton, in an attempt to either stop potentially islamaphobic voters from voting for her or to switch them to the Trump ticket. It is believed that the Trump campaign ran up to 50 000 niche-targeted Facebook ad variants daily during the campaign.

Journalists use social media as a primary source

Journalists have quickly adapted – they now regularly use tweets as source material for their stories, in certain cases forgoing the need to contact the person for clarification or context.

Bloggers are the new opinion leaders

Once seen as wannabe journalists or zealous whack-jobs, bloggers have carved out a space and legitimacy that has transformed the media landscape. 'Experts', 'specialists' and commentators now have their own online platforms – in both written and the fast-growing podcast formats. Their opinions count, and politicians are as likely to be seen in a basement or garage recording a podcast in a studio made from egg-box crates as they are to be seen at the swanky head office of a multinational media giant.

It's a quick (and cheaper) way to campaign

Social media campaigns – both the organic and the carefully curated – are much quicker to pull off than campaigns that rely solely on traditional (old-school) media. The Ice Bucket Challenge in 2014, for example, was an awareness and fundraising campaign for amyotrophic lateral sclerosis (ALS, also known as motor neurone disease or Lou Gehrig's disease). In the US, funds were raised for the ALS Association, although, ironically, they didn't actually conceptualise the campaign or its accompanying hashtag, #IceBucketChallenge. The campaign went viral across the globe as people shared online videos of themselves having buckets of iced water poured over their heads to raise money for ALS and then nominating their friends to follow suit. It was a bit of a gimmick and what some refer to as 'slacktivism', but the campaign raised more than $100 million in its first month.

The rise of social and online media has brought with it a whole new army of experts, consultants and teachers. Tertiary institutions now offer full degrees or catch-up courses. Anything else you may want to know can be found on Google or YouTube. So here we're not going to give you the rules, tips and techniques of using social media. Instead, we're going to share a few of the ideas and tactics political communicators use to campaign and to both boost and defend their candidates and parties.

Know when (and how) to respond to a story (and attacks)

For years the daily news media cycle went like this: the morning newspaper broke a big story which was then covered on talk radio and radio news bulletins. If the story was big enough, it made the evening TV news. No longer. Live news sites, online editions of newspapers and blogs have changed all that. But the real disruptor is how social media and citizen journalism have propelled that once metronomic tick of the daily news cycle into a whirring 24-hour buzz.

Like a tornado, under the right conditions a social

media attack can form in a matter of minutes, leaving you with little time to decide how to react – or whether to react at all.

Good political communicators have learnt not to over-react or respond prematurely. They tend to have two types of barometers to judge when to respond. Some wait for the story to reach a critical mass or to begin trending before assigning it importance and choosing a response. Others watch for when commentators, journalists or even important opponents begin to share, retweet and comment.

At that point they will choose a defensive or offensive tack. Depending on circumstances, the defensive route might include an apology or an explanation. The offensive approach might be to fight back and attempt to dominate the narrative online – or at least to muddy the waters and render the whole discussion opaque. Some teams even have scores of supporters and staff who can be quickly rallied to a timeline for deployment.

Planned attacks are almost impossible to shut down, but often well-meaning people are the multipliers and accelerators of those attacks. If, for example, an 'influential' person on social media is spreading damaging information, then you should consider sending them a private message explaining your position in an attempt to get them to self-correct. Public shaming has become de rigueur on social media. Frankly, it doesn't make you or your organisation look good. Rather contact the person privately and try to get them to fix the error first. If your organisation has been tagged or the comment is on a platform that you own and the individual does not self-correct after you have contacted them privately, then you should correct it yourself. However, the best outcome on social media is when you have reached out to your community of social media users and they respond on your behalf and correct inaccuracies without you having to do so.

Bell Pottinger's coordinated PR campaign using (among others) fake pro-Gupta Twitter accounts, also called Twitter bots, took garden-variety Twitter rage and attacks in South Africa to the next level in 2016/17. Thousands of fake accounts were created with the specific aim of providing support to the pro-Gupta lobby, giving voice to pro-Gupta narratives and savagely attacking anyone perceived to be an enemy or obstacle to their cause.

Use real-life humans as online personas

People like interacting with people. It's part of being human. Far too many organisations tweet and post in the third person, a problem exacerbated by a tendency to use language that is too formal or careful for the medium in question.

In 2011, President Barack Obama announced that he'd be personally tweeting – his staff had obviously been running his account up until then – and that his personal tweets would be identified with the initials '-BO' at the end of each message. That approach has gained traction both in the world of politics and within corporates.

It's a great idea, but it's not without risks – particularly in South Africa, where some politicians have already been publicly shamed and disciplined by their party for online comments deemed inappropriate or offensive. Politicians now find themselves caught between an online rock and a virtual hard place: they can be themselves online, warts and all, and risk offending someone, or they can hide behind bland accounts that serve as nothing more than online billboards for them and their party.

Think first, get advice, don't panic

In 2011, the *Sunday Times* ran a front-page banner headline story accusing the Western Cape government of a dodgy communications tender. (Months later, a Public Protector report made it clear that there had been no wrongdoing.) A front-page lead story was big – and bad. At 5 a.m. that Sunday morning, Nick was discussing what to do next with Helen Zille by text message.

He had made a series of suggestions of the steps we could take when Helen said, 'No, I'm going to say that I will resign if there is any corruption.' Nick understood that she wanted to make the strongest statement possible to assure people that there was no trace of corruption. But, equally, he knew this would whip up the trolls and make our political opponents rabid. So he replied, 'No, definitely don't say that – bad idea.' Her response? 'Too late.'

For the next six months we were at war, fighting off a

multipronged attack from whoever wanted to see the back of Helen Zille – and they weren't in short supply.

Communicating on social media and staying out of trouble isn't rocket science. If you follow the rules of good manners you learnt at school, you'll be just fine:

- Don't tweet or post before you think.
- Don't post in anger.
- Don't overreact.
- Don't respond to anything and everything said about you.
- If you have any doubts, ask someone else for their opinion – or just don't post it.
- Remember: once it's up, it will never ever go away.

And one rule you hopefully would not have learnt at school:
- Don't tweet or post after you've had a few drinks.

There's a meme that perfectly expresses our view on social media best practice:

Only say things you would say to your grandmother
Don't be a dick
Don't feed the trolls

Have a sense of humour

When DA Leader Mmusi Maimane made a public admission that he'd voted for the party of Nelson Mandela in the

1990s, Mayihlome Tshwete, the politically mischievous spokesperson for the Department of Home Affairs, tweeted:

> **@MTshwete:** IEC needs to explain how Mmusi voted for Mandela at age 14…we need answers.

It didn't take long for Tshwete's tweet to explode into a hashtag meme: #ThingsMmusiDid, an irreverent and bitingly sarcastic parody of Maimane's achievements and history:

> **@Thulani_Dlamini:** #ThingsMmusiDid teach Biko about Black Consciousness

> **@khabo1:** He was there when that dude decided to let the dogs out #ThingsMmusiDid

> **@Eusebius:** He was a waiter at The Last Supper. #ThingsMmusiDid

> **@TheBusy_95_Chi:** #ThingsMmusiDid passed matric with 783 distinctions…

> **@majokamenzi:** #ThingsMmusiDid captained the ship that brought Jan Van Riebeeck

Once social media whips itself up into a viral frenzy, these sorts of things have a life of their own. DA national spokesperson Phumzile van Damme countered with:

> **@zilevandamme:** The thing about ANC peeps starting #ThingsMmusiDid, is that if we do a #ThingsZumaDid we won't have to make things up, because, well, Zuma.

We can't help but think that this was a missed opportunity for Maimane to win a few hearts and minds with a self-deprecating yet clever tweet on the meme.

During the 2017 German election, Christian Lindner, the new leader of the resurgent Free Democratic Party whose campaign was in part built around his movie-star good looks and charisma, came face to face with a video from Stern TV of his pimply 20-year-old self spouting clichéd aphorisms and wearing a gimmicky cow-patch tie. The clip immediately went viral.

Lindner didn't miss a beat and tweeted:

> **@c_lindner:** Thanks, #sterntv. This used to be start-up culture 1.0 in 1997

Unsurprisingly, his self-deprecating tweet went viral and only added to his appeal.

Know where people are getting their news, and how it's playing

Save for tabloids, newspapers are being read by fewer people every year. And while radio and TV have their place, more and more people are getting their news online: on their Facebook or Twitter timeline or from digital editions of newspapers or media sites.

If you're only reading news in newspapers you will find yourself disconnected from the *other* public narrative. And just like print media, social media editorialises, repackages and takes sides. So you need to know more than what is in the news – you need to know how that news is playing online.

Keep an eye on journalists

Journalists are on social media to watch the world (including politicians) pass by, to keep an eye on trends and breaking news, and to scour for new stories. But they are also people. They have moods and feelings. They make friends. They have interests and passions. Just as it sucks you in, so social media sucks them in too. That's why social media is also a great way to get to know journalists.

The following are some prominent South African journalists' Twitter handles and tweets:

Carol Paton (@politicsblahbla)
'I love JZ unplugged'

Andisiwe Makinana (@AndiMakinana)

'And the Cape Town weather changes. It's suddenly overcast and looks like it may rain. ** My son cracked our 20l bucket when he turned it into a drum. 😌'

Richard Poplak (@Poplak)

'I left my iPad on a @FlySafair flight traveling from Johannesburg to Cape Town. Went to the ticket desk and laid out my stupidity in graphic detail. Twenty minutes later, I had my iPad. Properly impressive.'

Rebecca Davis (@becsplanb)

'Just ate my third hot cross bun of the day. Soon my outer junk status will match my inner junk status'

Just by following them you can get to know what they think and feel – about life and about the stories that make them tick. But it's also a genuine way to build rapport, to offer insights and useful information, and ultimately to even forge relationships with them.

Everyone is a journalist – be aware

Social media has also made everyone with a smartphone a 'citizen journalist'. There's a photographer at every corner and a recording device in the queue behind you. We're not advocating paranoia, but just warning that, should you wish to make a name for yourself or grow your organisation's profile, that comes with a price – and that price is public restraint over what you say and do.

On more than one occasion, police officers have been photographed sleeping on duty and the photos have been posted online. In the days before social media they might simply have dismissed the allegation or attempted to wriggle out if it. But now facing immediate and credible evidence, napping cops are likely to be in for the high jump.

Break news

While citizens across the globe, in the face of newsworthy events, regularly break news online, Twitter and Facebook are now becoming useful platforms for politicians and companies to announce their own news, thereby controlling the timing and tone of the announcements:

Julius Sello Malema (@Julius_S_Malema):
The achitect of Gupta corruption Mr Malusi Gigaba has unduly granted them South African citizenship. Read for yourself...

Sohaib Athar (@ReallyVirtual): Helicopter hovering above Abbottabad at 1AM (is a rare event) followed by...

> Uh oh, now I'm the guy who liveblogged the
> Osama raid without knowing it.

> **Redi Tlhabi (@RediTlhabi):** I've been on twitter
> ALL day yesterday AND gave birth during day;
> contractions..whole gamut...naturally. Joke on u
> 😂😂

> **Jim Hanrahan (@highfours):** I just watched a
> plane crash into the hudson river in manhattan

> **Eskom Hld SOC Ltd (@Eskom_SA):** Kusile's
> first unit is on the grid.

Stay on message but platform specific

The last piece of advice is some old-school media advice that works just as well for social media. Just as common sense tells you that you shouldn't submit a lengthy op-ed article on economic policy to a tabloid like the *Daily Sun* for publication or a photo of your neighbour's ongoing parking indiscretions to *Business Day*, the same thing goes for social media.

Every channel has its own purpose, personality and target market.

Don't copy and paste the same message, thought or idea on every social media platform you occupy. Not only does this make you look clumsy and stupid, but you will also lose credibility and the trust of the people with whom you are trying to connect.

For example:

- Put the full text of your announcement on your website.
- Load the 30-second infographic-style video on Facebook.
- Instagram the photos from the launch event.
- Tweet the best lines from your leader/CEO.
- Facebook Live the launch event.
- WhatsApp your clients to give them a heads-up to watch.
- Use the intranet to keep your team in the loop.
- And link them all up so people on Twitter know where to get the full text, people on Instagram know how to see the video, etc.

5

Crisis communications

'QUEEN STREET MASSACRE'

In the three years Nick spent heading up media for Auckland city in New Zealand and as chief of staff for the mayor of Auckland, this was the biggest media crisis he faced. Take a second to picture the South African equivalent: reading 'ADDERLEY STREET MASSACRE' on the front page of the *Cape Times* would, without doubt, be a shock.

Fortunately for Nick, this particular *New Zealand Herald* front-page story was about a plan to remove sickly alien trees from Auckland's main street and replace them with indigenous saplings!

All crises are relative, but all organisations will face one sooner or later. And South African political parties are no exception:

- The ANC has faced Nkandla and Gupta state capture.
- The DA has had to deal with Helen Zille's colonialism tweets.

- The EFF has had to address charges of tax evasion and fraud against leader Julius Malema.

Whatever the causes of these crises – or even the culpability of the organisations stuck in the middle of them – you can be sure that communications teams have spent countless hours trying to un-break eggs. The nature of politics means that political communicators experience more crises per capita than your garden-variety communications professional. We've taken the hits and felt the pain, but we've learnt a few things too.

There are two equally important parts to surviving a crisis: preparation and management. Here are the steps to take to be ready for and to get through any crisis:

Crisis preparation

1. Identify your crisis team in advance
This is the first step in any crisis, and should preferably already be in place when a crisis hits. Assemble a core team of decision-makers and essential services, including, at least, the following:
- An on-site decision-maker who does not need to refer up for decisions
- Subject-matter experts
- Media communications professionals, including a designated spokesperson
- Legal experts

- Stakeholder communications (whomever is important to you and your organisation)

Decide on a physical location from which to run joint operations – somewhere for the team to be physically based during the crisis. This proximity is essential for the fast-moving, ever-changing environment.

2. Identify the spokesperson

Choose the person who will be the primary spokesperson. Keep a list of back-up spokespersons and technical experts if necessary. Make sure all of them have as much professional media training as they might need in advance of any crisis.

Choose someone who can handle stress. In 2010, Kylie Hatton was the City of Cape Town's spokesperson when police and the city's anti-land-invasion unit clashed with Hangberg residents who had been preventing authorities from dismantling shacks on a firebreak on the slopes of the Sentinel in Hout Bay. She was doing a live radio interview from the scene when there was an almighty bang. Asked what was happening, she calmly said, 'No biggie, our car was just hit by a rock,' before moving on without skipping a beat.

3. Identify your stakeholders

Who are the internal and external stakeholders that matter to your organisation? Make a contact list and regularly check and update it.

4. Anticipate crises with a robust system

While doing a series of debriefs of various media cock-ups and crises in Auckland, Nick and his team arrived at a seemingly self-apparent realisation: someone in their vast organisation, somewhere, always knew, in advance, that there would be a particular problem. And for a host of reasons – a manager who disagreed with or ignored them, lack of confidence in coming forward, broken telephone – the executive of the organisation never got to hear about it in time.

So they designed a system that turned crisis planning on its head with this simple proposition: if something goes wrong and you knew about it and didn't tell us, then you take full responsibility for the consequences of that problem. Every single department was afforded a weekly forum to brief the communications team on potential problems. In turn, the communications team categorised each problem with a traffic-light code on a spreadsheet called the Media Issues Register:

Red	Contentious
Amber	Significant
Green	Business as Usual

Alongside each issue, the team noted the essentials that would give the executive a high-level understanding of the potential problem and the contingencies planned in the case of media attention:

Issue:	One sentence that crisply explains the issue
Date:	When this problem will happen or whether it is ongoing
Executive:	The senior executive responsible for this line function
Official:	The ranking official responsible
Comms person:	The person who will manage the issue in the media
Tactics:	Whether the organisation will communicate proactively or wait to respond reactively
	The full details of all communications undertaken and planned
	Who will be the spokesperson
	What media have already reported on this or are interested in the story

The Media Issues Register immediately became a mainstay at the executive committee meetings of the Auckland City Council and, after Nick introduced it back home in South Africa, a permanent fixture on the agenda for the cabinet meetings of the Western Cape government. The beauty of the system is that it gives busy leaders a quick overview of every potential problem in their organisation and the surety that the media risk is under control. An unintended but useful consequence of the system has been to reverse-engineer organisational problems long before

MEDIA ISSUES, EVENTS REPORT (CONFIDENTIAL)
as at 1 January 2018

PART ONE OF THREE - CONTENTIOUS ISSUES

No.	Code	Issue	Date	Executive
1	1 Contentious	NATIONWIDE LOADSHEDDING Scheduled shut-downs begin on 1 February. This is an operational necessity – failure to do so will place the nationwide grid in jeopardy.	Starts 1 March	CEO
2	1 Contentious			

PART TWO OF THREE - SIGNIFICANT ISSUES

No.	Code	Issue	Date	Executive
1	2 Significant	NEW POWERPLANT DELAYED Medupi will now only come on stream 2 months later than expected – due to unforeseen engineering delays.	Now/ ongoing	Head of Operations
2	2 Significant			

PART THREE OF THREE - BUSINESS AS USUAL ISSUES

No.	Code	Issue	Date	Executive
1	3 Business as usual	ROUTINE KOEBERG REPAIRS Reactor will be shut down for 3 days for routine repairs. No impact on grid.	25 February	Plant manager
2	3 Business as usual			

Official	Comms person	Communication tactics
John Smith	Pam Naidoo	Proactve campaign. Minister to hold national press conference. Liaising with office for a date. Advertising campaign currently being prepared – delayed by 2 weeks. FAQs complete and loaded to website. Stakeholder comms need attention. Full social media campaign + analytics are ready.

Official	Comms person	Communication tactics
Sipho Hlope	Marie Garstecki	Proactve. Still awaiting details from engineers – then will draft press release. Press release scheduled to be issued on Monday. Marie is briefed with a generic technical holding statement if story leaks before then. Minister's office briefed so that they are ready to field the political questions.

Official	Comms person	Communication tactics
Anna Swart	Lindiwe Malatsi	Reactive only. Holding statement & FAQs ready for release if requested only. Monitoring social media for opportunistic activism.

they get to the media. Premier Helen Zille would often call up officials – in the middle of cabinet meetings – instructing them to sort this out or fix that problem.

5. Rehearse

Think of crisis rehearsals like a building's fire drill – and for the exact same reasons. Walk into your office one day, gather everyone together and announce a scenario. And then see what they do. Repeat until they get it right.

Crisis management

Remember that a crisis comes in many forms. Some will happen in an instant and be resolved the same day, while others will drag on for months. The duration of a crisis might affect your timing and tactics, but the following crisis management rules apply.

1. Assemble the crisis team at the operations centre

For a short-term crisis (where everything happens in hours or days), the team should staff the operations centre continuously for as long as the crisis continues. For longer-term crises, it is essential that the team still meet regularly to share information and make decisions: this could be a daily hour-long team meeting or even a weekly status meeting.

You should have a back-up system in place in the event of a crisis happening out of office hours, including a pre-agreed arrangement on how decisions and tasks are managed remotely until the team is next in the same room together.

2. Assess the crisis situation and gather all available information

Make sure you have access to all information: experts, databases, technical information, etc. and that information can always be verified and substantiated. Compile and update crisp, credible, on-message answers to frequently asked questions (FAQs) on an ongoing basis. If possible, publish these FAQs online as soon as possible.

3. Act (communicate)

Here are the golden rules for communicating in a crisis:

- The first is the old adage: tell it all, tell it fast and tell the truth. With one addition: tell it yourself.
- Decide how you will source ongoing credible and verifiable information about the crisis. In other words, know the facts.
- If you or your organisation has made a mistake (or worse), then admit it – upfront. This is the first step towards re-establishing credibility and confidence with the media, your stakeholders and the public.
- Don't panic.
- Never ever lie or obfuscate the truth.
- Don't let the lawyers make the final decisions. They are notoriously risk averse – in some cases, to the detriment of the communications required.

- If you ignore the situation, it will only get worse.
- Don't communicate until you are ready to do so, but don't wait too long.
- As soon as the crisis breaks, get the spokesperson (and back-up and technical experts) rehearsing what you want to be saying, but – more importantly – rehearsing the answers to all of the tough questions they might face from journalists.
- And make sure they anticipate and practise new questions as the story evolves.
- If the organisational leader is not the crisis spokesperson, make sure the leader is also seen to be leading and taking an active, hands-on role in dealing with the crisis. People want to see their leaders leading in times of crisis.
- Determine who needs to be communicated with – who are the key stakeholders and how do you communicate with them?
- When dealing with complex, multifaceted crises, make sure that editors and senior journalists are briefed on the background, context and details of the crisis to help them better understand your decisions and actions.
- Understand that sometimes it is not enough to rely on the free media to communicate your message. Sometimes you will need to buy advertising space to get your message across. Just be aware though that big, splashy full-page apologies, for instance, notoriously piss off journalists, who see it as an act of arrogance.

4. Keep your team in the loop

While you are busy letting the world know what happened and what's next, make sure you keep your team and decision-makers updated. WhatsApp groups are probably the best platform for sharing information with multiple people in a crisis period.

5. Vasbyt

No matter the nature of the crisis and no matter how carefully you've prepared and responded, either the media, the public or stakeholders are not going to react the way you want them to. So sit tight. Stick to your messages. Tell it all, tell it fast and tell the truth.

Managing social media in a crisis
By Sarietha Engelbrecht, social media expert

The only thing that spreads faster than celebrity baby news on social media is public outrage. A small issue can quickly get blown out of proportion and turned into a full-scale social media crisis. With the right preparation and strategy in place, you can speedily nip issues in the bud. In fact, social media can serve as a useful tool to help you quickly identify and handle issues that might damage your brand. Here's what to do:

1. **Use a monitoring tool:** You should always be tracking certain keywords, hashtags and handles on social media, especially your own name, as well as those of your competitors. A monitoring tool allows you to easily see when people are talking about you, even if they don't tag you in the post.
2. **Have a social media crisis management plan in place:** This should contain guidelines for identifying the magnitude of a crisis, roles and responsibilities, and a communication plan for internal updates. The plan should also include up-to-date contact details for critical employees.
3. **Set thresholds:** As you monitor certain words, this will guide your actions and help you know when to escalate something to crisis status. According to social media management platform Hootsuite, if you see less than five negative mentions per hour, you can compile

these in a report for senior management to review at the end of the day. However, if there are more than 10 negative mentions per hour for three consecutive hours, you should call the head of marketing on their mobile phone and initiate your crisis management plan.

4. **Act fast:** Anger and frustration can escalate quickly. The longer you wait to respond, the more a matter can spiral out of control. Most companies take way too long to respond to an issue. Act as fast as you can to contain negative sentiment.

5. **Acknowledge:** People hate feeling ignored. The real-time nature of social media allows you to immediately and publicly acknowledge an issue while you work on a more detailed response. People often just want to feel heard, so acknowledging that you take note of their post and that you are going to get back to them with more information could stop them from making any further posts until you've had a chance to respond in full.

6. **Pause all scheduled posts:** Nothing makes your company seem more tone-deaf than continuing to post as per normal in the midst of a crisis. You don't want to seem like you're ignoring a problem, so if a crisis unfolds, pause all planned posts until the worst is over and you have figured things out.

7. **Respond where it first originated:** If people are slagging your brand on Twitter, it is no use posting a statement to your Facebook page or company website. You have to respond where the negative sentiments originated.

8. **Post relevant updates:** Silence only fuels a fire and gives people room to speculate. Post relevant updates as soon as you have them to keep people informed, even if they are short updates.

9. **If possible, take it offline:** When you respond to people directly, keep it short and try to avoid back-and-forth. A good rule of thumb is to never send a third reply. A third reply is an argument, not an answer. Try to move the discussion to private messages, try to get their contact details, or offer them an email address or phone number as a way for them to get in touch with you.

10. **Own your mistakes and apologise:** If you are wrong, take full responsibility and apologise. Put together a well-thought-out and sincere public statement and let a reputable and senior enough person in your company speak on behalf of your brand. If an issue occurred on your private account, it's up to you to own the issue and to apologise to the public directly. Show compassion and remorse, don't be defensive and don't try to justify your actions.

What not to do

- Don't delete negative comments: This will only enrage people more. Facebook has a helpful feature that allows you to hide comments, which means only the commenter and their friends will see it. Try to avoid deleting comments and blocking people.
- Don't take it personally: Don't get emotional and don't feed the trolls.

Case study:
Paul Edey and St John's College –
How *not* to communicate in a crisis

Faced with a crisis surrounding a teacher found guilty of using racial slurs at St John's College in Johannesburg, headmaster Paul Edey called in to Bongani Bingwa's show on Radio 702 to clarify why the teacher was not suspended despite considerable public outrage. This interview is an illustrative example of how not to communicate in a crisis. As you read through it, pay attention to how Edey:

- does not tell it all or tell it fast;
- seemingly does not take responsibility for what happened as the first step towards re-establishing credibility and confidence;
- panics – five seconds of silence on the radio is skin-crawling stuff;
- obfuscates the truth – Edey later apologised to Wits professor Sarah Nuttall for 'completely and inappropriately invoking her name', after Nuttall denied she was involved in this process; and
- clearly did not anticipate and practise any of the likely or probable questions.

Bingwa: Alright, the story that you would have heard throughout the afternoon is the decision by St John's College to not suspend a teacher that they have found, through an independent investigation process, through an independent hearing, that they found guilty of a racist incident and they've decided not to suspend this teacher and they said that they are taking a reconciliatory approach. Joining us on the line is the headmaster of St John's College, Paul Edey, and of course you want to explain your side of the story. Good afternoon to you.

Edey: Bongani, thank you very much for the opportunity, I really appreciate it. Obviously this incident and this process has caused a great deal of upheaval and upset and I understand that. Our first priority is our students and to look after their welfare. I just want to reiterate that this process has taken a long time, regrettably a very long time, but it was handled by an independent senior counsel and the decision was made that the master ... the teacher was guilty and that ... that ... that he ... a letter of final warning should be granted and—

Bingwa: What was he guilty of?

Edey: He was guilty of making stereotypical racial remarks.

Bingwa: What are those?

Edey: There ... a number of remarks that were made ...

Bingwa: Such as ...?

Edey: Well, comments about [five seconds' silence in response] referring to ... to race but—

Bingwa: Explain. Be specific. What did he say to those boys?

Edey: [three seconds' silence in response] Bongani, I

can assure you that the school is committed to a process of transformation.

Bingwa: Paul Edey, you've come onto this show to give your side of the situation. You found this man guilty, you say, of what I'm asking, what did he say?

Edey: I didn't find him guilty, Bongani, he was found guilty by an independent—

Bingwa: Sure, I accept that. The process found him guilty of what? What did he say to those learners?

Edey: [five seconds' silence in response] They found him guilty of making a stereo … stereotypical remarks.

Bingwa: What was that statement?

Edey: It was statements referring to boys on race.

Bingwa: What did he say? Do you not know it? Do you not have a record of it?

Edey: I do have a record of it.

Bingwa: What did he say? Take us into your confidence. Let people understand what exactly it is this independent process found him guilty of. What did he say to those learners?

Edey: Bongani, there was a comment about boys …

Bingwa: Tell me the comment.

Edey: … doing well on … in tests and … and … and doing badly because they were black or doing well because they were black and …

Bingwa: Did he say to those learners that they were doing well academically only because they sat next to white boys?

Edey: No, that was not one of the comments.

Bingwa: That was not one of the comments.

Edey: No. A lot—

Bingwa: Verbatim, please. Can you tell me what he said?

Edey: [seven seconds' silence in response] That 'You've let the side down by doing well in the test', to a black learner.

Bingwa: Which side? So he was saying he's let black people down?

Edey: [three seconds' silence in response] Yes, but—

Bingwa: Is that what he said?

Edey: That's what he said.

Bingwa: And you find that merely stereotypical?

Edey: Bongani, I don't find ... the school is adamant that it is ... abhors racism and bigotry. We are ... we have put in place a whole set of processes for transformation and diversity, we are involving our pupils and our teachers and our parents in conversations, we've engaged Dr Sarah Nuttall from Wits to begin those conversations ...

Bingwa: Sir, with respect, with respect, you have a teacher who's come and told a group of learners that they've let the side down for doing well, which suggests he expects them to do badly, and you have allowed that teacher back into the classroom and you're now coming onto this radio station to tell us you abhor this kind of behaviour. Are you kidding me?

Edey: Bongani, this was a decision given to us by an independent counsellor. We—

Bingwa: So you have no responsibility.

Edey: [indiscernible] There … [indiscernible].

Bingwa: You will throw those learners into the lion's den because the independent process said so.

Edey: We are not throwing any learners into the lion's den. We have counselled those learners through the process, we have given them psychological support and some of the facts that have been put out into the media are simply wrong.

Bingwa: Alright, Paul Edey from St John's College, what are your thoughts? It's merely a stereotypical incident.

Conclusion

The skills taught in this book are a curious mix of science and chaos. There are things you can control (which this book is about) and things you cannot (which this book helps you respond to), but ultimately there is something intangible that holds it all together: the art of being a good communicator, a good spin doctor. And the key to that lies between the lines. It lies in experience and wisdom, which you gain from trial and error, knowledge accumulation and practice. This book may have taught you the method, but to learn the art takes dedication, commitment and time. You can make a big difference to how you communicate by following our rules, but there are lessons we simply cannot teach, such as timing, attitude, persistence and focus. Likewise, inherent skill – some people have it, others do not.

That is not to say you should despair over your lack of experience. Take these lessons and use them consistently wherever and whenever you can. But also know that when

- you are in a hole and everything seems to be getting worse;
- you make an almighty mistake and someone prints it;
- the crisis seems too overwhelming;
- no message seems to work;
- the interview is a disaster;
- you post something online that you immediately regret; or
- the campaign falls flat on its face,

we have experienced the same, and much worse. These are the scars and moments that, collectively, bring wisdom and judgement. Don't be too hard on yourself when you fall. We all have.

In the face of all these techniques and systems, it's also easy to lose sight of the fact that, in a world where contestable and fake news vies for space with the real deal – all instantly and simultaneously on your timeline – professional communicators hold more power than ever before. While it is naive in the extreme to assume that the truth will always out, it is incumbent on the ethical and principled among us not only to tell the truth, but also to challenge the lies and liars wherever and whoever they might be. One can only hope that the sudden and spectacular demise of Bell Pottinger serves as a timeous reminder of the consequences for those who use spin for the wrong reasons.

Appendix: Essential tips

... for writing a good press release
- The opening paragraph must explain what the news is, what your position on that news is and why it is important.
- The body must provide argument and analysis, context, and evidence.
- The title must be short, punchy and accurate.
- Try to include an action step.

... for when a journalist contacts you
- Don't be rushed into anything – buy time to think and compose yourself.
- If they're from a newspaper, ask them to email the questions to you.
- If they're from a radio station and are calling you for a sound bite, find out what they're looking for from you and then buy some time to prepare.

- Find out their deadline, or agree to an extension, and then stick to it.
- Stay on message, no matter the line of questioning.

... for a radio interview
- Prepare and practise your responses by speaking them out loud.
- Rehearse an answer to the worst possible question you can imagine.
- Find out who will be interviewing you.
- Find out how much time you will have.
- Stay on message, no matter the line of questioning.

... for driving issues
- Stay on message.
- Make sure there is a binary position.
- Select the correct opponent.
- Is there real conflict?
- Be first.
- Protect your issue from theft.
- Make sure your issue is sustainable.

... for surviving social media
- Don't tweet or post before you think.
- Don't post in anger.
- Don't overreact.
- Don't respond to anything and everything said about you.

- If you have any doubts, ask someone else for their opinion – or just don't post it.
- Don't tweet or post after you've had a few drinks.

... for being crisis ready
- Identify your crisis team in advance.
- Identify the spokesperson.
- Identify your stakeholders.
- Anticipate crises with a robust system.
- Rehearse.

... for surviving a crisis
- Assemble the crisis team at the operations centre ASAP.
- Assess the crisis situation and gather all available information.
- Don't panic.
- Don't let the lawyers make the final decisions.
- Don't ignore the situation; it will only get worse.
- Don't communicate until you are ready to do so, but don't wait too long.
- Keep your FAQs updated.
- Stay on message.
- Always tell it all, tell it fast and tell the truth.

Acknowledgements

We want to thank all of our friends, colleagues and the experts who contributed their thoughts and ideas to this book:

Russel Brueton
Gavin Davis
Sarietha Engelbrecht
Kylie Hatton
Anthony Hazell
Jan-Jan Joubert
Lauren Kent
Cecelia Kok
Tony Leon
Wulf Pabst
Jan Scannell
Bettina Solinger
Greg Wagner

A particular thank you to Gareth van Onselen and David Maynier for their typically inspired and thoughtful views, and to Pam Zolkov for transcribing Nick's lectures. We also want to thank all of those politicians – from all parties – as well as editors, producers and journalists who contributed their knowledge and experience, and who have preferred to remain behind the scenes.

And a final thank you to Bronwen Maynier for giving structure to and making sense of our ramblings.

NICK CLELLAND

CAPE TOWN, FEBRUARY 2018

RYAN COETZEE

LONDON, FEBRUARY 2018

Index

Achmat, Zachie 82
Ackerman, Raymond 68–69, 82
action steps, in press releases
    37, 44
advertising 14, 114
African National Congress *see* ANC
AIDS *see* HIV/AIDS
ALS Association 92–93
ANC 8, 80–81, 105
apologies 94, 114, 118
arms deal 76
Auckland 105, 108–109
availability 35

Banting 83
Bell Pottinger 16–17, 95, 126
'Better Together' message 8–10,
    13–14
billboards 55–56
binary position, of issues 74–75
Bingwa, Bongani 119–123
bloggers 92
Bokamoso video blog 91
brand strategy
    communication of
        brand promise 12–16

definition of brand 5
ethical standards 16–17
personality 11–12
promise 6–8, 10
slogan 8–10
values 10–11
vision 6
Branson, Richard 39
brevity 35, 57–58
bribes 34
'brown envelopes' 34
Brownson, Charles 30
bumper stickers 54
    Bush, George H.W. 53

Carlisle, Robin 66
Carville, James 58
'Chatham House Rule' 26
chicken suit 53
citizen journalism 93, 101–102
Clelland, Nick
    in Auckland 105, 108
    DA 19–20, 27–28
    DP 1–2, 55
    jet for Thabo Mbeki 84–87
    TV interview 65–66

at Western Cape government
48–49, 96, 109
Clinton, Bill 53, 58
Clinton, Hillary 78, 91
clothing for TV 65–66
CNN 54
Coca-Cola 16
Coetzee, Ryan 1–2, 6, 68, 75–76
conflict 68–69, 74, 76, 77, 80, 81, 83
context 32, 43–44, 114
corruption 79–81
creating news 21, 39–49, 102–103
creativity 14–15, 52–56
  crisis communications
  case study 119–123
  essentials tips 131
  importance of 105–106
  management of crises 112–115
  preparation for crises 106–112
  social media and 116–118

DA
  allegations about Gerald Morkel
    19–20
  arms deal 76
  brand strategy 6–10
  creative communications 53–56
  crisis communications 105
  luxury ministerial vehicles 80–81
  Nkandla 77, 80
  press releases by 47
  relationships with journalists 22–24
  video content 90–91
  volume of communication 15
Davis, Rebecca 101
'day in the life' 53
deadlines 31, 58–59, 130
De Lille, Patricia 76
Democratic Alliance see DA

Democratic Party see DP
dinner table conversations 70–72
DP 1–2, 22–24, 55, 68
'drag and drop' 61
'driving issues'
  checklist for 74–78
  concept of 67–73
  essentials tips 130
  examples of 68–69, 78–87
  finding issues 87–88
  themes vs issues 72–73
'Durban Poison' posters 55
Duvenhage, Wayne 82

Economic Freedom Fighters
  see EFF
Edey, Paul 119–123
editors 21–30, 31, 114
EFF 77, 106
elections
  in Germany 99
  social media and 91–93
  in South Africa 1, 27–28, 55
  in US 5–7, 10–12, 53–54, 58, 78, 91
email 57
eNCA 65
Engelbrecht, Sarietha 116–118
ethical standards 16–17, 126
e-tolls 56, 82
events, media alerts for 47–48
eye contact 64–65

Facebook 23, 90, 91, 118
face-to-face meetings 23
family dinner table conversations
  70–72
FAQs 113
'filling the silence' 63, 119
'Fire Manto' bumper stickers 54

'for attribution as …' 26
frequently asked questions *see* FAQs
German election, 2017 99
good manners 38, 97
graphs 45
Gupta family 16–17, 37, 79, 95, 105

Harksen, Jurgen 19–20
Hatton, Kylie 107
Health Professions Council of
    South Africa 83
hierarchy, in media houses 30, 31–32
Hill-Lewis, Geordin 28
HIV/AIDS 54, 75–76, 82
honesty 10, 29, 34, 59, 62, 113, 119,
    126
Hootsuite 116–117
Hout Bay 107
humour 97–99

Ice Bucket Challenge 92–93
immigration 78
inaccuracies in reporting 29, 94–95
in-person interviews 60–64
Instagram 90
integrity 10
interviews 60–64
'in volume' 14–15, 58
issues vs themes 72–73
    see also 'driving issues'

jet, for Thabo Mbeki 84–87
journalists
    crisis communications 114
    essentials tips 129–130
    first contact with 56–58
    from perspective of 30–38
    relationships with 21–30, 34–38, 59
    social media and 92, 100–101

Kennedy, John F. 64
lawyers 113
Leon, Tony 53, 55, 84
Lindner, Christian 99
listening 62
'Lunch Time Rules' 26

Maimane, Mmusi 91, 97–99
makeup, for TV 64
Makinana, Andisiwe 101
Malema, Julius 77, 89, 90, 102, 106
marijuana 55
Martins, Ben 37
Mazibuko, Lindiwe 80
Mbalula, Fikile 75–76
Mbeki, Thabo 54, 75–76, 84–87
Media Issues Register 108–112
Media Relationship Management
    Programme 22–24
Merkel, Angela 90
Mexico 78
ministerial vehicles with blue lights
    80–81
monitoring tool, for social media 116
Morkel, Gerald 19–20
Murray, Brett 82

New National Party 53
news cycles 31, 49–50, 51, 93
newspapers 31, 100
New Zealand 105, 108–109
Nixon, Richard 64
Nkandla 77, 79–80, 105
Noakes, Tim 83
Nuttall, Sarah 119

Obama, Barack 95
'off the record' or 'background'
    26–27, 36

ombudsmen, of newspapers
    29–30, 32
'on message' *see* staying on message
'on the record' 26, 36
operations centre for crises
    107, 112–113
opponents, selection of 75–76
OUTA 82
over time, staying on message
    15–16, 58

paid communication 14, 114
Pan Africanist Congress 76
Parliament 54–55, 77
Paton, Carol 100
Perlman, John 20
personas, online 95–96
petrol price regulations 68–69, 82
Pick n Pay 68–69, 82
Player, Ian 82
playing cards 54
podcasts 92
police officials 102
political communicators 20–21,
    94, 106
politicians and social media 50–51,
    89–93, 95–96, 102–103
Poplak, Richard 101
'Post-box to Parliament' campaign
    54–55
posture 64
Press Code 27
press conferences 38
press ombudsman 30, 32
press releases 37–38, 40–47, 129
Public Protector 80, 96
public shaming 94–95

quantity *see* 'in volume'

radio 42, 50, 58, 60–64, 119–123, 130
Radio 702 119–123
Ramaphosa, Cyril 39
rehearsals 112
relationships with journalists and
    editors 21–30, 34–38, 59
respect 38
Royal Institute of International
    Affairs (UK) 26
Russia 91

SABC 28–29
SAfm 20
shaming 94–95
short sentences 41–42
silence, awkward moments of 63, 119
Sky News 25
'slacktivism' 93
slogans 8–10
smiling 62, 65
social media
    citizen journalism 101–102
    creating news 102–103
    crisis communications 116–118
    essentials tips 130–131
    humour 97–99
    journalists and 91–92, 100–101
    online personas 95–96
    platform specific communications
        103–104
    politicians and 89–93
    responses to attacks 93–95, 96–97
    sources of news 100
sound bites 56–57, 58
South African Social Media Landscape
    Report 90
specialisation 31, 33
speculation 25
spokespersons 107, 114

stakeholders 107, 114
'state capture' 16–17, 37, 79, 105
statistics, in press releases 45
staying on message 12–14, 58, 61,
    74, 103–104
Steenhuisen, John 53
Stern TV 99
St John's College 119–123
storytelling 73, 80
strobe effect 65–66
Sunday Times 96
Sunday Tribune 55
Sun Tzu 5
sustainability of issues 77–78
'sweeteners' 34

teams, for crisis communications
    106–107, 112–113
television *see* TV
themes vs issues 72–73
#ThingsMmusiDid 98–99
three 'A's of communications
    disasters 89
tone, of press releases 44–45
Trump, Donald 5–7, 10–12, 39,
    78, 89, 91
trust 29, 36, 64–65
Tshabalala-Msimang, Manto 54

Tshwete, Mayihlome 98
TV 50, 64–66, 99
Twitter 17, 23, 89–90, 95,
    98–103

'unattributable' 26
United States (US) 5–7, 10–12,
    53–54, 58, 64, 78, 91

values 10–11, 16–17, 33
Van Damme, Phumzile 99
Van Schalkwyk, Marthinus 53, 54
video content 90–91
visions 6
volume of communications
    see 'in volume'

wall between US and Mexico 78
Waters, Mike 20
Western Cape government 13–14,
    48–49, 96–97
WhatsApp 104, 115
'white monopoly capital' 16–17

YouTube 90

Zille, Helen 7, 89, 90, 96–97, 105, 112
Zuma, Jacob 33, 77, 81,

The authors

Nick Clelland is a communications expert and strategist with experience in the most aggressive media and public environments. He is the CEO of Resolve Communications, a lobbying and advocacy agency operating in South Africa, and a former MP for the Democratic Alliance. Nick has directed political communications operations on three continents: he was director of strategic communications for the Western Cape Government in South Africa, headed up media communications for the Auckland City Council in New Zealand and, in Britain, was part of the media team for the Liberal Democrats 2005 general election campaign. He is also an experienced communications trainer and a member of the teaching team at the International Academy for Leadership in Germany.

Ryan Coetzee is a South African politician and political strategist, who has served as special advisor to UK deputy prime minister Nick Clegg and was the 2015 general election director of strategy for the Liberal Democrats. In 2016, Ryan was director of strategy for the campaign for the UK to remain in the EU. He previously served as an MP in South Africa, as CEO of the Democratic Alliance, as the party's general election campaign chief, and as chief advisor to Western Cape premier Helen Zille.